CW00496987

Why you are Australian

Also by Nikki Gemmell

Shiver
Cleave
Lovesong
The Bride Stripped Bare
Pleasure: An Almanac for the Heart
The Book of Rapture

Why you are Australian

A LETTER TO MY CHILDREN

NIKKI GEMMELL

Fourth Estate • *London, New York, Sydney* and *Auckland*

Fourth Estate
An imprint of HarperCollins*Publishers*

First published in Australia in 2009 by Fourth Estate,
an imprint of HarperCollins*Publishers*, Australia
ABN 36 009 913 517
harpercollins.com.au

Copyright © Nikki Gemmell 2009

The right of Nikki Gemmell to be identified as the author of this
work has been asserted by her under the *Copyright Amendment
(Moral Rights) Act 2000*.

This work is copyright. Apart from any use as permitted under the
Copyright Act 1968, no part may be reproduced, copied, scanned, stored
in a retrieval system, recorded, or transmitted, in any form or by any
means, without the prior written permission of the publisher.

HarperCollins*Publishers*
25 Ryde Road, Pymble, Sydney, NSW 2073, Australia
31 View Road, Glenfield, Auckland 0627, New Zealand
A 53, Sector 57, Noida, UP, India
77–85 Fulham Palace Road, London, W6 8JB, United Kingdom
2 Bloor Street East, 20th floor, Toronto, Ontario M4W 1A8, Canada
10 East 53rd Street, New York NY 10022, USA

National Library of Australia Cataloguing-in-Publication data:

Gemmell, Nikki.
  Why you are Australian / Nikki Gemmell.
  ISBN: 978 0 7322 8959 1 (pbk.)
A823.3

Cover design by Natalie Winter
Cover image © Sheridan Nilsson/Wildlight.net
Endpaper image of Tamarama Beach © Sheridan Nilsson/Wildlight.net
Author photo by Justin Creedy Smith
Typeset in 11/17pt Minion by Kirby Jones
Printed and bound in Australia by Griffin Press
70gsm Bulky Book Ivory used by HarperCollins*Publishers* is a natural, recyclable
product made from wood grown in sustainable forests. The manufacturing
processes conform to the environmental regulations in the country of origin,
New Zealand.

5 4 3 2 1   09 10 11 12

To my country

PART ONE

1

The three of you emerge from Sydney's airport and squint into the hurting light of January. I've rarely seen any of you squint — you were all born in London and aren't used to such hard Antipodean light. But it's a brightness I dream of in England, our land of no-shadows, where the sky's so low, often, it almost touches the chimney-tops.

You see, I'm photophiliac; I'm a lover of light. And as I stand beside you all, my three little pommies, I feel tall, spined up; my skin drinks in this light like the desert does rain. I am unlocked. But you, Thea, eighteen months, throw up your hands in horror; you, Lachie, eight, and Ollie, six, screw up your faces at the assault of it. None of you appreciate this brightness. For you come from a different land, and your country is not mine.

Why are we here?

To learn why you are Australian. To know this land. The three of you were born in London's Chelsea and Westminster Hospital yet your Aussie father and mother chose to give you Australian citizenship over British. You need to understand that choice, to be introduced to this country you've only visited fleetingly up till now.

We have left your daddy and our home in London's Notting Hill for three months. We escaped the depth of a northern-hemisphere winter that's flinched not only by cold but by recession, to stretch our limbs in the light of Australia. You boys have leave from your small, private London school to join a big Aussie state one for a term.

We're doing this to be with my grandmothers, ninety-nine and ninety-six, because it is time; I'm sick of visiting them briefly every couple of years and then saying goodbye all too quickly again. They need to know their great-grandchildren, and you need to know them. We are doing this to be with grandparents and aunts and uncles and cousins; to be marinated in family. To live for a while under a tall blue sky; to see what that does to you.

And we are doing this because home fills my heart, and I need you to understand why. But is this sweet, sad craving that whispers endlessly through my veins stopping me from viewing Australia objectively? Would I ever, really, want to live in it again?

We're all here to learn in this place.

2

I've lived in England for twelve years and the homesickness
is corrosive now; it gets worse, not easier, every year.
Australia — its sky, smell, sun — holds my heart hostage.
The egalitarianism of free sunshine. In Britain the rich buy
it. They jet to Elsewhere in December and February and,
most cruelly, August. It's the summers over there that do
me in. England in winter is the England of my imagination,
but when it's overcast in London for every single day of
August, well, my heart just about cracks with frustration —
for you children as much as anything. Every childhood
needs its basting in sunshine.

So here you are now, my three luminously pale little
Londoners, standing outside Sydney airport and squinting
into this blast of light and not liking its hardness one bit.
You boys in particular are true Brits. You have accents
sometimes veering into Cockney ('li'l' instead of 'little',
'bo'l' instead of 'bottle') and an embarrassment when, in
front of your friends, your funny old mum calls wellies

'gumboots' and felt pens 'textas' and crisps 'chips'. 'Mu-um, you're in England now; you have talk *English* not *Australian*.'

Your Aussie parents had a hold on you until you began school, then the accent slipped along with everything else. I'm still wondrous at the way you boys pronounce 'mummy'. Coax it out of you sometimes just to hear the fabulous difference of the word; the pronunciation I can't get my tongue around.

My father tries endlessly to turn his beloved grandchildren, on the other side of the world, into Aussies. Coaches them on the phone to say 'g'day', jokingly admonishes them whenever a vowel is sounding too Brit.

My father. Another pull to home.

He visited the Notting Hill mews house that we used to live in, our beloved shack off Portobello, which once housed the market's vegetable carts. And at the end of a wonderfully meandering day of kids and chinwags with stallholders and revivers in coffee shops, he retrieved my hammer from its toolbox and fixed our old, wide floorboards, hammered in all the thick Victorian nails that were coming loose. As his work was drawing to a close I began to cry, and felt like a ten-year-old; I cried with all the intensity of childhood. Because I suddenly felt very alone in this vast city, and wanted my dad, and mum, with me very much. Someone to look after me, because I spend so much of my time looking after everyone else.

To have my family around us all now, in the country that has haunted me for so long, has become a river of yearning through all my London days.

3

For you Notting Hill lads, Australia is a land of cliché. You're wary of it from your faraway country so benign at the other end of the world. Aren't completely sure you want to join this mad adventure, where Mummy is stepping outside her life for a little while and dragging you along with her. You've protested. Will miss your London world too much. Your friends, house, car, Wii. Don't particularly like the sound of your parents' homeland. For it consists of a few certainties: deadly creatures, many, the country teeming with them, in the oceans and rivers and the bush, in the swimming pools and garages and under the houses and possibly in your slippers which must be shaken out, every morning, without fail. Other certainties: absolutely no rain. And this eternal, glary, hurting light.

(There's one lovely certainty even if it's swamped by all the scary ones: sparkly blue water. Vast expanses of it. 'That's Grandfather Bob's swimming pool!' you, Ollie, exclaimed excitedly several years ago, when the plane from

London flew over Sydney Harbour. Because everyone in Australia has pools, that's what you'd been told, and they're all outdoors, and very big.)

A country of cliché for you; a country of the imagination for me. And I need to soak myself in it again. I dream, on arrival, of doing something similar to the Aboriginal woman who shed her Christianity by walking down to the dry riverbed and rubbing sand all over herself.

But with light.

Scrubbing myself with it. Shedding the northern hemisphere. Washing away England. Low cloud and reserve and pessimism and dull teeth, even in kids; washing away the layers of grime that have accumulated on a country too old, creaking, crammed; too weighted by its history, its glories too far in the past.

There's a seismic shift in me, in my early forties; I'm turning away from my London home. It's been such a happy, glowing place for so many years but I'm ready for something new. This feeling is dangerous and wrong on so many levels but rupture is good, replenishing. I had forgotten that as motherhood and marriage grew over me, shutting me in.

4

I'm ready to see my country with fresh eyes. And I need to show you children. Can't wait to see your intrigued approach to this foreign, unfamiliar land.

'Stars only happen in videos,' you, Lachie, declared a few years back. That decided me. *This has to be done*, I kept telling myself, before England settles over you all completely and you never want my country; before you learn to look down upon it — and its people — like so many Brits do; before you are irritated by the Australian accent. And of course, you never do see stars in London, just a vague orange glow from all the light pollution. That breaks my heart. That *this* is your childhood.

It's time to show you the Australian sky. The night sky, the enormous high breadth of it, a vast canopy above you that's dark, properly dark, and weighty and rich. It's time to point out to you the Southern Cross and teach you all its emotional reverberations. And it's time to introduce you to an Aussie childhood. I want you to experience something of my own childhood for a little while, if possible; that feeling of being burstingly alive under a high blue sky, grubby feet and mozzie bites and bindi-eyes and all. I want you collecting cicada shells and eating fish and chips at the beach and squealing through sprinklers and swinging on a Hills Hoist.

Can we find that kind of world again? Will you end up glued to the telly and web games on your computer screen, just like your London life?

I have no idea. But achingly I want you to know what it is to be Aussie kids. Where playing barefoot is a signifier of freedom not impoverishment. Where a backyard's a given and not a luxury. Where sunshine and fresh food grow children tall. Where you know what a rash shirt is and a nipper, a Paddle Pop and a Boogie Board. Where you learn to swim that beautiful Australian Crawl and to smile when you talk; where you learn confidence and optimism and enthusiasm and reach.

'You're giving them a childhood,' murmured a London acquaintance wistfully when I told her of my plan. She's a Notting Hill wife enmeshed in a world of Miu Miu and Jimmy Choo, four cars ('one just for the freeway'), a full-time nanny, a weekend nanny and a housekeeper. She left her dynamic job when she had kids and has never gone back. She's imprisoned restlessly in her life; the dissatisfaction rattles around her, the yearning for something else.

'I feel like fear has dictated all my choices in life,' she said once.

In Thea's nappy bag I've slipped a farewell card from another girlfriend, Caro. She has scrawled inside, 'Adventure makes the soul sing and your heart want to explode and your spirit soar into a world that suddenly seems huge again. Feel the freedom ...'

Yes, oh yes.

5

There's another reason for returning home: a particularly female one. It's to do with always trying to be the good mother, daughter, wife; with being the constant pleaser; with endlessly saying yes. Until you're worn ragged from it.

My love for you children, you darling children, is greedy, wild, voluptuous; since you've been with me it's like God has breathed life into the bellows of my days and everything has become warm, sparky, alive, light; it is a great, addictive incandescence and I am so grateful for it. And I love your daddy still, very much: his love, after twenty years of mateship, feels like an underground river deep and nourishing and strong right through me. It still works; and I am wondrous at that. And he still makes me laugh — the secret, I think.

Yet, yet.

I've never been more exhausted. The tiredness is now like some alien being that's nestled inside my body, sucking away all my energy. And I had so much of that once. I've relinquished control of my life; I no longer completely call the shots. My longed-for career as a novelist has softened as I try gleaning preciously selfish writing time around full-time motherhood; as I attempt, often unsuccessfully, to steal moments of blissful and necessary aloneness from everyone dependent upon me. That's four of you. One who, until recently, literally fed from my heading-into-middle-age body.

At times this tiredness dumps me like a wave in the surf, and I am, despairingly, 'beside myself'. And sometimes in those fretful moments I have to leave all of you, just get away, and grab an hour or so of solitude in a café down the road. Just to be by myself. Reclaim me. Remember the woman I once was. So I have the strength to go on.

You see, sometimes I don't recognise the woman I turn into; the one who yells at her kids and husband in a voice I've never heard before. Who is she? It horrifies me, yet I can't keep the ugliness locked away in a box; in the stress of the exhaustion she's sometimes unleashed and I'm ashamed but can't stop. I don't want any of you to see her. But you do, my loves, you do; and I know that the memory of her is something you will carry through your childhood and beyond.

So. As I face the endless routine of regular life, the washing machine and nappies and dishwasher and school run and squabbles over TV and what-will-we-have-for-dinner? and do your homework *now* and it's bedtime, come *on*, sometimes there's a dangerous yearning within me — wrong and selfish and greedy I know — for rupture. To crash change into my life.

Hence this trip. I don't know why but I feel like it could save me. I think it's the washing pile that's pushed me to do it the most. I can get the dirty clothes in the washing machine. I can turn on the machine. I can take the wet clothes out and put them over the radiators throughout the house to dry. I can pile the dried clothes on the floor. But sort them back into their drawers and cupboards? That defeats me. Until I have to do it, because that growing pile of clothes and towels and pillowcases and sheets becomes a volcano of exhaustion and lack of control and despair that threatens to erupt over my entire life.

> The need to go astray, to be destroyed, is an extremely private, distant, passionate, turbulent truth.
>
> Georges Bataille

6

Throughout my late teens and twenties I moved restlessly from landscape to landscape, gulping up fresh experiences, filling notebooks and journals with vivid material, swallowing up life. It was all fuel for my fiction. I lived in Sydney's Kings Cross and Darwin and the desert of Central Australia; went to Antarctica and all manner of continents; and then ended up, at thirty, in a single room on London's Fleet Street with an ex-boyfriend, Andy. Your father. And always with me were the words of Chekhov's consumptive narrator in 'An Anonymous Story': 'Life is only given us once, and one wants to live it boldly, with full consciousness and beauty.'

Oh yes, to live boldly and fully. I did. My heart was flung wide open, and there were so many knocks and bruises and stumbles along the way. The swamping of a broken heart again and again and again; the walls of my Kings Cross flat are still soaked in tears from a broken engagement and a cheating boyfriend and a lover who was accidently killed;

16

so much living crammed into those fraught, jagged, often bleakly alone years, so many tears that all this time later I can barely stomach the thought of living in that flat again.

And now, with your father, there is the grace of a settling. Though at times it feels like this new world is firming around me like concrete.

Does every wife, mother, woman feel this at some point? What is this rangy restlessness that undermines the shining days? Gabriel Garcia Marquez said that life obliges human beings 'over and over again to give birth to themselves'. But can women get away with that vicious selfishness within the demands of partnerships and marriages and motherhood? Who actually follows through with their distancing, their chip of ice?

I see some women, a generation or two older than myself, who have gone almost mad with the inability to break free; the failure to negotiate a way into being truly themselves. It's as if they have somehow stepped to the side of their own lives, and it's only in their later years that the enormity of that — all the ramifications — wells up in them. Then the bitterness comes.

God help me if I ever get to that.

Coco Chanel said 'my life didn't please me, so I created my life' and I've done that all through my adulthood and now, at forty-two, I want to give it another shot. Because at times I feel like a horse boxed up in its stable, constrained, unable to break free, kicking out.

7

'Is everything ... OK ... between Andy and you?' a few people have tentatively asked. Because it's obvious to everyone who knows us that he's crazy with love for all of you children. And to take you away from him, albeit temporarily, seems bizarre at best.

Yet he's strangely supportive of this plan; perhaps he knows that it's potentially replenishing for me and for the relationship, and that in giving me my freedom he's somehow, ultimately, binding me. Or perhaps (the bugger) he's just licking his lips at the thought of several glorious months of weekend sleep-ins, for the first time in eight kid-crammed years. The *intensity* of those years, and the prospect of a guilt-free reprieve ...

'If you're happy, the whole family's happy,' he says. And another time, with his beautiful, roguish smile, 'You're mad as it is. If I don't let you go you'll only get madder.'

My husband is giving me my freedom. It's been granted strongly and easily. We have confidence in each other; Andy trusts me and I him. It's a recognition, from both of us, of the restorative nature of the plan. Other couples do it. Sometimes it works, sometimes not. A friend who's disappeared several times from her own marriage says the sojourn can founder 'if the wife is too dependent'.

Dependency. Perhaps, as a woman, it all has to do with control and the loss of it. The American former Secretary of State, Madeleine Albright, spoke of how her ex-husband's tastes became her own in their twenty-three years of marriage: that after she left him she rediscovered the fact she didn't like beef — even though for years they'd eaten it almost every single night.

Oh yes, I know something of that, and perhaps Andy does too. It in no way diminishes our love; it's just the way it is between partners who've been together a long time. I no longer have cereal sometimes for dinner, or even skip the meal if I don't feel like it; I no longer stop shaving my legs in winter. Madeleine Albright regained her control by getting divorced. Perhaps I can do it by stepping outside my life, my regular London life, for a while.

'I've become weak from pouring whole bags of sugar in my tea,' a Pintubi elder told me years ago in the Central Australian desert. I know what he means. It's like I've had it too sweet over the past decade of marriage, have become as soft as a pocket. Once I'd not only fill up my beloved old ute with petrol but change its tyres; now, we have a family sedan and I do neither. I've become dependent and need to toughen up. Become an Aussie chick again: reclaim self-sufficiency, the woman I once was.

> Learn to free yourself from all things
> That have moulded you
> And which limit your secret and
>   undiscovered road.
>
> Ben Okri, 'To An English Friend in Africa'

God knows if it's possible within the thick of married life.

PART TWO

8

So here we are, freshly arrived in Sydney; the four of us in a line, husbandless and fatherless. Squinting into the blinding light with little idea of what's ahead. I feel taller already. Empowered by the prospect of solitude and the gift of control, the chance to call all the shots with you kids — become a tight little unit — with no one to counter what I'm doing. Empowered by the delirium of return, the dazzling Australia of my imagination that awaits us. And as I stand there strong, my chest opening out into the lovely repairing sunshine, my eyes adjust and I look around properly.

And my heart sinks.

At the scrappiness of the airport's exterior. What happened? Where's my sparkly city? I used to walk out to a lovely phalanx of paperbarks and breathe them in deep — now, it's a ratty concourse cluttered with mobile fast-food vans and an outdoor seating area littered with cigarette butts. What other major-city airport greets the world with such a sight? Where's the will to impress? The sense of pride, reach? The overwhelming impression is … provincialism.

My heart flinches. Suddenly I'm overwhelmed by all the old uncertainties of the expat: the feeling that yes, you want to return for good, but can never quite bring yourself to do it. The will may be there but the question is when — and the when may never actually come.

I think of what I've left behind. Heathrow, tatty and worn and scrappy yes, but so dynamic, bustling, vivid — it feels like the great bursting hub of the world. The day before flying out I passed a fresh Banksy-esque painting on a Portobello wall of Prince Charles with his strained smile, in drag, on the loo — and that sums up London to me. Witty, untidy, irreverent, street, modern, creative, grubby, subversive and so utterly, gloriously alive. Exuberantly so.

In the window of a junk shop nearby was a penny-farthing bicycle — a penny-farthing! (Shouldn't that be in a museum?) Down the road was a huge grey-and-white graffiti portrait of Samuel Beckett's ravaged face. I changed my watch battery amid the clicking murmur of old clocks in a shop like something out of Harry Potter's Diagon Alley. Picked up you boys from your little school that has nothing in terms of facilities, but is giving you an extremely rigorous education in the Three Rs. When you do a project on castles, which you both have, we take you to visit several that are almost one thousand years old. Kew Gardens, the British

Museum, the V and A, the Natural History Museum: they feel like enormous treasure houses of all that the world has to offer, and they're right on our doorstep. In London, I still have wonder. I revel in a country that has not one but ten national newspapers, with all the diversity of opinion that encourages, all that jostling competitiveness and cheeky irreverence. The sheer vibrant tumult of it all.

And now this.

Fast-food vans and cigarette butts on the milkshake-stained, gum-strewn concourse of a country-town airport that couldn't care less. That's what Sydney feels like. The first impression, beyond the blinding light.

My heart flinches, oh yes.

9

How can I ever persuade Andy to one day call this Australia home again? Return: it stirs such complex, contradictory emotions in us both. He revels in his adopted city, the feeling that all the world is in London. What I've just landed in is not the airport of a sparky major player. What happened to Sydney's ambition and hunger, so dazzling and exuberant and flash during the 2000 Olympics? It's not Aussie cockiness any more, it's complacency. Everything around me looks tatty, dreary, shrunken, hemmed in by concrete and car parks. Perhaps, as Andy insists, the kids *would* be better off in London. Their world wider, their horizons brighter, their intellectual stimulation deeper.

I did not want Australia to be this. I've been haunted by my country for years and now need the reality to align with the projection and the memories. The loss of my country has tormented me. I don't want too much of a shock on this trip. Because I'm also seeing Australia through Andy's eyes and, for him, the great adventure of life is continuing — elsewhere. Resolutely so.

We've watched appalled from afar as beloved icons like *The Bulletin* magazine and the Gowings corner in Sydney have gone; as some of the nation's boldest thinkers — Robert Hughes, Germaine Greer, Richard Butler — have fallen victim to the small-spirited culture of sneer through all-too-human failings. And now this: another nail in the coffin of return. A Sydney that feels like it's stopped trying, that's given up.

In despair I think back to a picture of you two boys I hold in my heart. To remind me why I'm going ahead with this mad trip, why I'm choosing to rupture the routine of your little lives so dramatically. It's an image from a brief moment several years ago, when I'd brought you back to Australia for a fortnight's holiday.

Late July. Sydney. The two of you running in delirious circles on Watson's Bay beach — without a stitch of clothing on. A huddle of Japanese tourists looks at you, bemused, as do I: for you're responding like true Londoners to Sydney's sharp winter sky. You're reacting to the land in an exuberantly physical, instinctive way — by flinging open your lungs to the sun and diving into the light. You smelled grubby, sweaty, vigorous; you never smell like that in London. My heart flooded with love. My dear little pommies, basted by sunshine! I just wanted to breathe in the smell of your squirmy bodies.

It's the smell of my childhood, the smell of home. And it was like you were suddenly using muscles I'd never seen in action in England; you'd become bolder, brighter, wild with delight.

My heart cracked as I stood there watching the children you might be, if you were raised in another place.

10

To Bondi. Fast.

Of course, the place we've chosen to stay in the early days of our trip is that world-famous beach so many Brits lay claim to on Christmas Day. And we are Brits too, in many ways now, doing the comforting English thing.

I can feel the four of us uncurling as we arrive at the ocean and breathe in the slap of its briny air. The dazzling beauty of Bondi's clean, golden sand and the exuberant roar of its blue surf overwhelm the clutter of nondescript buildings and tourist tat that fringes it, thank God, and always will. Yes, it's magnificent, and we stare in wonder, and gulp it all deep.

This is what we came for.

'I know what they are,' you, Ollie, declare excitedly, pointing at people's feet. 'They're called flongs. People wear them in ancient Rome.'

So much to learn. And I'm an outsider now too, as wide-eyed as you children. We all walk too slowly to cross the road before the green man in the walk sign disappears. We all marvel at the letterboxes in brick walls detached from the blocks of flats. The cracked and worn roads. The concreters pouring the wet cement. The occasional bare feet. The myriad of bodies on display — old people, middle-aged people, a heavily pregnant woman in a tiny bikini — and the deep brown skin, particularly on elderly people. We watch the local children like anthropologists to find out the clothes you boys should be wearing: ah yes, rash shirts and baseball caps, surf T-shirts and trainers. Then head to the shops to kit up correctly, to become locals in this land, to disguise ourselves as Aussies even though we all carry Australian passports.

You, Lachie, drop a teddy you're holding for Thea and a woman stoops to pick it up.

'Thank the lovely lady,' I say.

'Lady?' she laughs breezily, 'I *wish*.'

I giggle with her. Love the Australian sense of humour, have missed it so much.

And of course, I completely forget about combating the light, drunk with the glory of sun and beach and sky after the grey of England for so long. We haven't even unpacked our suitcases before we're on the sand and running to the pounding surf, you boys stripped down to your underpants and Thea in just a nappy. We bask in it all — astounded, joyous, greedy, exhausted — until the light softens.

And by day's end we're lobsters. Pommy lobsters.
So much to learn.
Re-learn.

11

FROM: NOTEBOOKS
WHAT IS LOVED

The originality and vigour of the Australian language. Wussbag and squizz and bingle, shonky and tingle and dag. Esky, servo, ambo, tradie. Battler — and, at the other end of the spectrum, bludger. Stirrer and wowser. Trackie daks. Sloppy joe. Gummies and skidlids, cossies and clobber and togs. Catch ya later, cop ya later, ripper and beaut and ute.

'You'll get a paddy whack if you don't watch it,' laughs my brother to his kids. 'I'm just standing here making a nuisance of myself,' explains the girl at the shop counter yakking to her mate. "Ave a good one,' offers the bloke with the beautiful, suggestive smile at the drive-thru bottleshop where I buy your milk, Thea. I have no idea what he's referring to but I'm still giggling as I hit home. A woman watches you vigorously tucking into my food at a café and leans across with a

conspiratorial smile: 'My dad has an expression for that: she'll be good on the toot.' What can you do but laugh heartily in agreement?

Caboodle and cobber and conk, yakka and Woop Woop and nipper. Arvo and agro, barras and blowies. Dingbat and nong and dunny. Billy lids and larrikins. And a southerly buster, the thought of it, well, that's just about enough to burst my heart.

A Notting Hill mate giggles every time she hears me talking about a 'singlet' around the boys. In England, it's a 'vest'. 'It's like referring to a doublet,' she laughs. 'It sounds so weird, so old-fashioned.' A malingerer, perhaps, from the convict days.

The sign outside the Workers' Club that reads, 'After nine pm No Singlets, No Workboots, No Thongs.' People in Notting Hill wouldn't know what any of those mean.

'He couldn't fight his way out of a wet paper bag.' 'I'm as busy as a dog burying a bone in a marble floor.' 'May your chooks turn into emus and kick your dunny down.' 'She's a sandwich short of a picnic.' '... a brick short of a load.' 'He's got some kangaroos loose in his top paddock.' 'You're mad as a cut snake.' '... low as a snake's belly.' 'Pull the other one — it plays Jingle Bells.*' 'Full as a goog.'*

From Newcastle, on someone being drunk: 'He's as full as the last bus out of BHP on a Friday night.' And a new favourite, heard on triple j: 'I get into it like a showbag, mate.' Only an Aussie could understand the full emotional resonance of that statement.

1 2

So, to the exhilaration of a strong Australian shower — after years of snivelly English ones. Aussie expats stranded in England for too many years talk longingly of the vigour of the water they've left behind. Like the rain in Australia it's pummelling, and it's one of the things I look forward to the most. Who would have thought such a simple sensation — tough, hot water — could brim you with such euphoric pleasure?

Those first, heady days of return, after the initial shock of the airport. Drunk not just with sunshine but all the comforts of childhood: mountainous bowls of Nutri-Grain, beef that's not going to give us mad cow disease, Tim Tams, banana smoothies, Chocolate Montes, Paddle Pops. The greedy gluttony of arrival; and every time it's like this. Revelling in home.

Revelling in family. We cleave to my mum, who lives in Sydney, in those first days of arrival; she helps me so much. We cram into her car; wander the cavernous

Westfield Bondi Junction with her; buy supplies. I relish the extra pair of hands. She takes you boys to a movie and lunch while I sort out the basics for the next couple of months: a mobile phone and Medicare. (The latter I'm not allowed to rejoin, to my shock — despite paying Aussie tax I've been out of the country too long and will only be eligible when I move permanently back. 'Don't get sick, you lot,' I later joke.)

Having family around me to help with you kids is a revelation — I've never done parenting like this. The *ease* of it. It also makes me realise that there's such an intensity to the love Andy and I throw at the three of you in England — it's just us, and you, and no one else. In Australia you have unconditional love on tap: it envelops you instantly from so many different family members and you're blooming within it. It's so moving to see.

I'm cherishing those big, affirming rewards of return; and so many small moments too.

Tinned beetroot. Hamburgers with the lot. Fly screens. The smell of eucalyptus as the day softens into darkness. A tall night sky. *Stars!* Buttery, meltingly fresh fish. Fruit, in its correct season, that tastes fabulously of the past, that tastes as it should. The scent of frangipanis and gardenias.

But then again, lingering in the kitchenette of our serviced apartment at Bondi, there's also the unmistakably Sydney aroma of cockroach spray and baits. It's been years since I've smelled it and I smile through the irritation as I fling the windows wide; right, another creature for you boys to learn about. One I forgot to mention. You've never seen a cockroach in your lives.

You've never seen many of the other things that are going to be crawling all over you, stinging you, biting you, annoying you, throughout the next few months. I brace myself for all the horrors that will be reported back to your father and your classmates. 'Urgh, there's one of those biting things on me.' You, Ollie, had squirmed away in disgust on the first day of arrival.

That would be a fly.

And so the lessons begin.

We begin with the constant battle against the encroaching armies. The crash course is fast and furious: right, mozzie bites and stings and bluebottles and funnel-webs and redbacks and tourniquets and snakes disguised as sticks and ants that may end up in cereal but don't panic, they're, er, good for you. We're turning you into tough Aussie boys, all right?

Wide eyes on you both.

I hand you a dishcloth each — it's time to turn you into men of the future. But it's also something you have to learn in Australia: the importance of wiping surfaces clean, always. No wonder Aussies are so fastidious — several Brits have commented on it to me over the years. 'You Australians are all so *clean*.' We have to be, mate, we've been hounded from childhood; never leave food and crumbs around a kitchen sink or bench, never leave a sticky mess, always, scrupulously, wipe — or the invasion will begin, fast. Ants, flies, cockroaches, you name it … and you boys are terrified of the lot of them.

Britain is so benign in comparison. The only thing we have to worry about there is the stinging nettle, and nature most beautifully has provided a remedy — dock — that grows right alongside it.

13

'I miss Australia very much,' Nick Cave once said to the Melbourne *Age*. He lives in England's Brighton (remember that beach of timid waves and pebble-sand?) and he's also Australian. 'I have a feeling that a lot of my alienation has to do with the fact that I'm not living in the place I'm supposed to be living in,' he explained.

The place you're meant to be living in. And the situation's so complicated if your children were born elsewhere. What accent will they have? Where, exactly, is home? For all of you?

For me, in these euphoric early days of arrival, there's no question where home will always be. The land at the bottom of the world the ancient mariners dubbed so enchantingly *Terra Australis del Espiritu Santo*: South Land of the Holy Spirit. The land where the light bashes us (in England it licks). The land where we can sleep under the stars and be tickled by the air rather than huddle against it (the cold in Britain curls up in my bones like mould).

Where we can see the moon and the stars because the skies are properly dark ('The light pollution has bled away London's stars,' our Pakistani newsagent laments).

But I fear, my little ones, that both your parents have slipped into some expatriate's no-man's-land now: outsiders not only in England but our homeland as well. We wonder if we'll ever settle contentedly into Australia again — worry that we've entered a strange state of displacement where the euphoric memories of home cannot be reclaimed in the Australia of today.

Yet Europe will never quite hold me. Well, Paris, yes; but not England. What better city than the ravishing French capital to live with full consciousness and beauty? It assaults you with its beauty; I go there, often, just to … look. To bask. It's not a smiley city, it's never been that, but like a sullen lover it only makes me crave it more. I have a more sober, testy relationship with London, perhaps because I know it better. Paris embodies a common human hope that the world is more beautiful and romantic than it can ever be — aren't we all aspirational when we go to Paris?

They've been wonderful times, the best of times, in London. I've loved its rangy, red energy; the exhilarating feeling as I walk down the streets of Soho that yes, all of life *is* in this place. I've loved playing in history, the cobblestones soaked in blood and tears and fire and smoke — hundreds, thousands of years of it; I've loved the gracious beauty of Bath and the Lake District, the Thames on a summer's night, the cherry blossoms of a Notting Hill spring; but none of it, none, has entered my heart.

Because it is not my land and never will be. Because I'm not living in the place I'm meant to be living in.

Andy argues that creates a dynamic tension, keeps you on your toes, is an enormously creative space to be in. That we should be using the grate of it, the stimulation of constantly striving within it, of always evolving and moving forward within the great and glorious energetic mass of it.

Perhaps he's right.

1 4

We both love the freedom the expat's life has given us. In your homeland you can never completely escape your past but in exile you're a cleanskin. You can reinvent yourself, do what you really want to do. You can be, finally, yourself, for you're not being constantly judged and admonished by the people you grew up with. All of that can feel so closed and narrow-minded and claustrophobic. Anonymity — the anonymity of an exile — is liberating.

Once upon a time, your daddy and I ran away from where our lives were leading us, at an age when we shouldn't have been contemplating such things. I was thirty, and could see just over the horizon the frantic waving of a very sensible existence involving long-service leave, contents insurance and a proper fridge.

Your father was thirty also. This is when we set up shop in that tiny room on London's Fleet Street. When Andy's mother saw our reduced living circumstances she cried. It was all in her face: 'Two Australian professionals in their thirties — in this?' We'd reverted to laundromats and backpacks and bar fridges but were having an enormous amount of fun staving off adulthood. One day we'll go home, we vowed, and start cooking, and get a lawn mower and decide what we want to do with our lives. When we grow up.

In Europe, Andy and I reinvented ourselves. We were bolder and braver than we'd ever been back home. All the Aussie expats around us were do-ers, and it was infectious. We brought to our new land a restless, cheeky energy, a feeling we could do anything here, by ourselves: we could do what we really wanted to. And if we failed, well, no one had to know.

The Brits bought it. We've both had the best careers of our lives in England — perhaps because we didn't care as much. If something didn't work out, well, we'd just reinvent ourselves again. And now, whether we stay or go has become a question mark between your father and myself.

15

FROM: NOTEBOOKS

The astonishingly friendly naïvety (I've been in Europe too long). For example, the guy in the Bondi Bookshop after I enquire about the possibility of ordering books: 'Well, it might take a couple of days, or weeks, depending on what it is.' Right. The tyranny of distance, of course. Then I ask about Amazon and he's off, eagerly chatting on about how quick and amazing the service from Amazon US is. 'You should try it, you can get books in a week or less, it's so good. I use it all the time!' That sheer, impulsive Aussie generosity. He just wants to help — bugger his business.

The lovely, easy way the two women come up and engage with you, Thea, in the smoothie queue at the shopping centre (you are driving Mummy slightly bananas with your whinginess). The women can see it, and they're helping me out. Kissing you, cooing, doing 'round and round the garden' until of course you're giggling. 'I just want to eat her,' says one of the women, kissing your pudgy little hand. I smile in gratitude. It doesn't happen in London. I'd forgotten the tonic of friendly, open, optimistic people.

A prang. A car rear-ends another at a zebra crossing we're walking across. I flinch in anticipation of the storming out, the slamming doors, the yelling, abusing, the calling for witnesses. Both cars pull over. 'Hi,' says the driver who was hit, in a friendly, sympathetic tone, as she gets out of her car to survey the damage. The shock of the civility of it.

The man in the sandwich shop. I don't have the cash required. He doesn't take cards; the nearest hole-in-the-wall is a bit of a walk. 'Just give me what you've got,' he says amiably, with the most beautiful smile, 'no worries.' Such simple things, yet so rare in London.

I have to speak to an Australian call centre to get my mum's old mobile phone underway. I need to supply my reference number, which I have to hunt for because of course it's tucked away in a handbag not close. 'Don't hang up, please don't hang up,' I plead to the woman on the other end of the line. 'Why would I?' she replies, surprised. 'Take your time.' Friendly, matey, as if she has all the time in the world. I'm stunned.

The palaver to post your little drawing, Ollie, to your mate Gabriele back in London. You've stuck on two Paddle Pop sticks, and because of this I have to fill out a customs form, give a valid address, and back it up with ID. All because, I presume, those two ice-block sticks might pose a terrorist threat. Then again, why isn't Britain so rigorous?

16

I want a sense of possibility and reach for you children; the knowledge that you can be anything, do anything if you set your mind to it — and suggest to your father that you've probably got a better chance of feeling that in Australia. Life feels too opaque in England; too much about what school you went to and who you know. Still. Rudd climbed, Obama climbed; but I'm not sure the same glorious ascent could ever happen in the near future in England. The class system continues to feel so entrenched, on many levels; despite all the changes over the past century the world still feels 'sewn up' by a powerful elite.

That ridiculous, world-seizing, mind-boggling ambition of a Baz Luhrmann or a Germaine Greer or a Clive James feels fabulously Australian. None of them came from great privilege — they're from the bush or from suburbia — but the key, I think, is that no one ever told them they *couldn't*.

In the UK you're constantly kept in your place. Parents fight tooth and claw to get their kids into the 'right' school, knowing it will set them up for the next stage then the next, the 'correct' path of a successful life that takes you through an Eton or a Marlborough College and then on to Oxbridge. That's the Notting Hill goal. If you're rich, you can buy opportunity. In Australia, you can earn it.

I love the idea of a country that says you can be whatever you want to be, no matter what your background, as long as you have ability and work hard enough. America is that, and Australia. It rewards industry and talent; England still largely rewards like-minded people.

Andy's much less keen on an Aussie childhood for you all; he says I romanticise my homeland and will get a hell of a shock when I finally come to live in the southern hemisphere again; that I may well be one of those Aussies who turns on her heels in fright and heads straight back to London. We know a few.

I know that coming back for good won't be easy. Salman Rushdie in the *New Yorker* described exile as 'a dream of glorious return', and yet homecoming can be so complicated if it's to Australia. There's that Aussie element that enjoys cutting its bolshy expats down to size, and considers their achievements grubbied by the disloyalty of assuming that life might be better elsewhere. It licks its lips at the prospect of people coming home; wonders if it will catch them slinking in, tail between their legs. It's ready with the cynical smirk — 'Couldn't cut it, eh, Over There?' — while the travellers' truth may be simply: 'We're done. We know we should stay away longer but actually, we just want to come home.'

Why? Well, as an expatriate family in Europe our lives have never been quite 'proper'. There've been no weekends taken up with a cousin's birthday or a visit to Grandma and we never go to christenings and rarely weddings; for all those rituals belong to a grown-up world of responsibility and obligation and friendship mulled over decades, to a family life that's settled, stable, certain. Ours is not.

We move in an anchorless expats' world and know all too well the suspicions of school admissions secretaries who never quite trust we'll hang around, and Easters with just, well, us. In a hotel. We're a tight little pack of five, bound by blood and love and exile. It's lovely and lonely and one day it will have to stop. When we grow up, Andy and I joke, and get a proper life.

But our homeland — the land we glean from the media — can be so viciously the land of sneer. We balk at living among such small-mindedness. We watched from afar as Robert Hughes then Nicole Kidman were subjected to vicious, ugly-spirited attacks that from England only looked embarrassing — for Australia. Small people trying to drag larger people down. It just feels so … sour. What punishments were meted out for daring to shine a little brighter! Patrick White spoke of a similar ugliness in the fifties. It fills Andy, in particular, with horror.

But a friend has rattled me. He's a painter in London who fled Perth during the Menzies years ('they didn't celebrate difference then, it was so viciously narrow'). His grown-up daughter is well and truly a Brit — she's visited Australia yet has no emotional connection to it, never wants to live there, will stay in England for life. My mate flew to Perth a few years back and said it was the last time he'd ever return to his birth place: it's too hard on him now, England's his home, it's been so long since he left, Australia's the past.

I dread ever saying that.

17

'I am in love with moistness'

George Eliot, *The Mill on the Floss*

And I am in love with light. Lock me in the sunshine. It's a constant wish within the mewly days of England, where spring doesn't mean sunshine but mere brightness in the sky.

And lock me in the land. An Aboriginal friend, Michael Williams, told me once: 'You are born into the land, you have a sense of responsibility to it, you don't leave it.' I feel strong when I'm close to it, stilled, anchored. Doesn't everyone?

Living overseas has taught me that whitefellas can have just as fierce an attachment to the Australian soil as Aboriginal people. A woman from Yuendumu said once she feels sick, physically sick, whenever she leaves her land. I can't say that, but I do feel firmer, calmer, when I'm back in it.

In Australia, nature presses close — even in bustling, built-up, car-riven Sydney; it seems so fecund and jungly in comparison with London. Suddenly, here, I am seeing sky again, the sheer melodramatic sweep of it. Sunsets. The startling beauty of gum trees, the arrest of them threaded through suburban streets. The lushness of the city's undergrowth spilling out. I'm hearing a cram of bird noise in the mornings, a big raucous wallop of it and then later, in the still suburban heat, the shrill of cicadas. It all feels so close, teeming, alive.

All four of us are so sweaty here, our skin slippery from the humidity. Our hair is lank, my lipstick slides off, my watch strap feels too hot. Many people tell me the Sydney summers are changing because of global warming, and even Alice has a wet heat now. Blimey. The physical manifestation of the change is so obvious in ten short years.

I feel the thumb of nature everywhere in this country; wear it, quickly, like a mark. Mosquito bites clustering around my ankles, a deeply browned arm from driving the hire car and an insistent golden V at my neck. You, Ollie, call the salt water at Bondi 'spicy' because it feels so stinging and fresh. None of those meek little British waves thank you very much, demurely lapping at their pebbled shores. Nature is so insistent in this place.

One of Australia's most famous poems, Dorothea Mackellar's 'My Country', was originally published in London with the title 'Core of my Heart'. When I read that snippet it clicked: it's a poem of yearning, for her own soil. She is explaining her love of a foreign landscape to the English.

The love of field and coppice,
Of green and shaded lanes,
Of ordered woods and gardens
Is running in your veins.
Strong love of grey-blue distance
Brown streams and soft, dim skies —
I know but cannot share it,
My love is otherwise.

I love a sunburnt country,
A land of sweeping plains,
Of ragged mountain ranges,
Of droughts and flooding rains ...

The emotional swell of those four lines! In England I want Australian light like a lover, ache for it. Ache for the life I had under it. It felt like my world back then was so close to the earth, so free and wide and unencumbered: that I could jump in my ute and gun it halfway around the continent healing a broken heart; that I could go bush on weekends with just a swag and notebook and a shoebox full of tapes; that I could drive for five hours to visit a beloved girlfriend then the next day drive back.

In London our life is so hemmed in, crammed, congested: close buildings, people, overpasses, train lines, roads. Entire schools are squashed into one small house, some with no outside playing space. Farms are small, clouds are low, windows with their net curtains are set meanly into pebbledash. When you leave the cities town tumbles upon town with scarcely any breathing space between them and so much of it feels meek, crumbling, cowed. I've changed over the years of London living; stay in Notting Hill now and rarely venture beyond it. With three kids it's often just too hard. Once I was in love with the great zoom of life; England, I sometimes fear, has knocked it out of me.

18

One of the main reasons for this trip is to dive into nature again — with you city-swamped kids. We're staying in Australia from January until Easter, the time of the ringing light. I'll be writing too, if I can, while being a single mother to you three kids (many are doubtful, including myself). I'm equipped for work, always am, the laptop and notebook forever with me, wherever I go, slipped into all manner of handbags and backpacks.

We've begun with the salty slap of Bondi, then will move two hours north to Newcastle's Lake Macquarie, at the foot of the Hunter Valley, where you boys will go to school with your cousins, Jaiden and Leonardo, for a term. Near the end of the trip we're heading to a spot near Cairns where Andy's parents now live. He'll be joining us for the final three weeks — 'to repatriate you back to the motherland,' he smiles.

My body is craving Australia. A replenishing. I need to run my palms over the smoothness of a eucalypt trunk, crush its leaves and smell them deep, breathe in the scent of them on an evening breeze. I need to stand under a southern night sky and be woken in the morning by an insistent sliver of light stealing through a curtain gap, calling me out. I need all of it, all, to spine me up. Need a renovation of my serenity, and I can't get it in London.

If I'm in England for too long the craving for the bush becomes intense, until my life is held hostage by it. Over the past twelve years, on book trips back to Australia, I've stolen snippets of time whenever I could to immerse myself in the land again. In Melbourne's Flinders Park I've walked by the shin-bone beauty of a lone ghost gum among the olive-greens of the English trees and pressed my palm to the cool, silvery starkness and held it and held it there for a very long time as gladness spread through me. On an expressway near Brisbane I've opened the car window and breathed in a bushfire and been intoxicated by it. I've stood tall on hill country that feels like it's on the roof of the world. Bathed in a bath filled with dam water the colour of milky tea. Walked through the jumping grass of bleached landscapes, marvelling at the dry flick of the grasshoppers. Had red dust soft as flour claim my boots. Driven through cathedrals of trees arching over roads with dirt thick on the dashboard. Climbed through bush taut with sound. Swum in shockingly cold creeks, silky soft dams, silty lakes, spicy surf.

And always marvelled at the gloriously wide spill of stars that you, my children, haven't yet seen in this land, because at the start of this trip I'm pouring you into bed each night, utterly exhausted, before the sun has properly set. But it's good exhaustion, the best, because all three of you are filled with fresh air and running and climbing and swimming and light. The soles of your little feet are toughening, the flesh is sitting tighter on your frames, your skin is goldening up; it's as if you've been basted in honey and I can't stop staring at the loveliness of it.

And when you're all vastly asleep I sneak outside and just stand there and gaze into the sky, my heart swelling with an enormous, glittery gratitude. At the lovely familiarity of it all. The constellations of the night sky pointed out in childhood and countless campfires in adulthood — Orion, Taurus, the Seven Sisters, Sirius, the Southern Cross and its pointer stars, Alpha and Beta Centauri. I'd forgotten how deeply comforting all that familiarity — and beauty — is.

In the Northern Territory several years ago I bought a swag out of sheer nostalgia and wanted instantly to rub its newness in dirt, to stain it permanently with the land. Goodness knows what we'd ever do with a swag in London, or where we'd put it. We don't have a laundry there, let alone a shed. Or grass.

'What's a childhood without grass?' demanded an old Darwin mate, Jess, in amazement. 'And bindi-eyes?'

I didn't have an answer.

It's so hard in England to find the wild places; it's all so meek and tamed over there. You have to travel to the farthest edges of Britain — northern Scotland or Wales or Cornwall — to be slapped in the face by nature. In Australia, gloriously, it's all so close.

And then, only then, can your eye rest.

1 9

That other reason for return: family. And it's a trickier one.

Who was it who said you can never go home twice? In my case it's been exhilarating to escape the weight of obligation for so long: several decades of it, as family members have aged and new cracks in relationships have appeared and been patched up, or not; as elderly relatives have moved into the homes of their children; and as new generations have been born. I've missed most of it. Since my early twenties I've been elsewhere, with only brief sojourns back. I've become addicted to packing up and running. It's always felt flighty and free and kind of glamorous. I hate conflict, prefer to escape than confront. Home always got in the way of whatever I wanted to do with my life; it felt too judgemental, diminishing, constraining, too *known*; it would always begin to tighten around me until I had to break free of it and refresh myself with change, again and again and again.

The poet Les Murray remarked of his own homecoming: 'I think I went back there in order to go mad.

I think if anyone goes home, that's what they're looking for. They're looking to go mad ... the past, if it's not dealt with, comes back and insists on being dealt with.'

Now, I'll be immersing myself in the past as soon as we hit Lake Macquarie. Most of my immediate family live around it. I have little idea what to expect; am exhilarated in one respect and dreading it in another. That family will close over me, pull and tug and demand, sap me in a way I don't want. It's all an experiment.

Once I was neophiliac, moving restlessly from landscape to landscape, and I have that chafing again — but I'm a mother now. And perhaps at some point I just have to embrace the mystery of being settled; find the courage to surrender to a new way of life surrounded by stillness, and family.

20

Returning to Woollies with the drinking cup Thea has plucked from a supermarket shelf and is holding/stealing as the groceries are being totted up. I only realise in the carpark, and am dreading the checkout encounter when I take it back. Why? Because I've been in Britain too long and have learned a flinching, a cringing kind of defensiveness, an instinctive 'it wasn't my fault'. What ensues is a cheery conversation between all of us — the checkout chick, the woman she's serving, the man behind her — about little monkeys accidentally stealing things. It's sensible and straightforward: casual, friendly, full of laughs. There's none of the Brit 'edge'.

'His smile would crack the frowns off a hundred faces,' said Bree, the wife of Sergeant Brett Till, the tenth Australian

soldier to die in Afghanistan. What is it about the Australian smile? So wide, easy, indiscriminating: infectiously beautiful.

The 'Public Defender' page in the Daily Telegraph *(subheading: 'Fighting For You'). Members of the public write in with their stories of being treated shonkily by the corporate world and government departments, and the bloke who runs the page tries to resolve the situations. In the UK it's different: the thinking is that the ruling class wins and always will and you've got no real hope. It's a matter of perception, and it's disempowering over there. It breeds tremendous frustration with authority. In Oz, it's more about a fair deal, if possible, no matter who you are: keeping everyone in check, especially those bastards at the top. An attitude that perhaps stems from convict days.*

Every car patiently queuing at a green arrow behind the car waiting to go straight ahead from a left-hand lane where everyone else wants to turn left. No bipping, no aggression. As a driver, I haven't witnessed that for years.

Indicating when you're turning corners and changing lanes. Brits often don't. You have to second-guess. It's about consideration, politeness, as much as anything.

21

Can I protect you better in Australia, my darlings? Give you a more secure life? There's so much Down Under that can damage you — snakes and spiders and jellyfish, crocodiles and sharks, the sun, floods, fire.

But there are different terrors in England, and some have rubbed up close to your childhood. For example, your bizarre, tremulous, nursery graduation, Lachie, on 7 July 2005. Normally such a happy occasion, but on this morning there were all the empty seats because so many expected parents were stranded by the four bombs that had exploded almost simultaneously on London trains and buses, which we all often use. Public transport was at a stunned standstill; mobile networks were jammed; landlines were down; no one, at that stage, knew exactly what had happened.

The resonances are still with us all: when you boys first heard the bips of a Sydney traffic light telling pedestrians to wait before crossing the road, you both gasped in horror, 'It's a bomb!' and clutched me tight.

Then there was our trip a couple of years ago to Disneyland Paris. Pre-Thea. A train from London took us directly to the theme park via the tunnel under the English Channel. And of course there was that familiar scratch of travel anxiety, post-9/11, as we passed through security at the London train station: in a corner was an Arabic-looking man with 'NYC' on his jacket and bulging gym bags, being questioned intently by three policemen. My belly did the little twist it always does now when international travel is endured. 'Please let this man not be on our train,' was my selfish, silent prayer. I'm not proud of this wish, which was also, by extension, 'Please let him blow up someone else's train, if that is what he is going to do.'

You see, ours was a train of children, the only one of the day that goes directly from England to the gates of Disneyland. There wouldn't be an adult travelling alone upon it. Would Al Qaeda really focus on such an innocent target? I cannot answer that. But it was a trainload of mainly affluent Brits travelling to a symbol of American cultural imperialism in a country that had just banned the wearing of Muslim headscarves in schools. With the most emotive cargo imaginable: a nation's young.

And we all know effective terrorists have to have a great eye for a story. A bomb in the tunnel under the English Channel — immolation and drowning — what could be worse?

22

Andy was reading my thoughts, and waved your old passport photo, Lachie, under my nose. It never fails to make me laugh: our five-week-old son looked like a younger version of Tony Soprano and bore no resemblance whatsoever to the beautiful boy before us now. My husband, God love him, is always trying to jolt me from my fears; he's always implying that I'm imagining too vividly and worrying too easily, that I just need to relax.

'Women who write feel too much,' the poet Anne Carson said, and I've wanted to tell Andy this more than once in my defence — See? This is why I feel fluttery and fragile at the direction in which the world is heading; it's darkening around us. Can't he feel that? Wouldn't it be safer in Australia?

'God no. Look at Bali.'

(Actually, I did tell him once about that Carson quote. 'Yes, Sylvia,' he replied, adding, 'that's for the gas,' with his wonderfully dry Australian smile, as he threw a box of matches at me.) I never used to live like this. Motherhood has changed me; a cautiousness is closing over me.

But we unclenched as soon as we'd settled into our sleek Eurostar carriage — the man in the bomber jacket couldn't possibly be among all the chattery, cluttery, bouncy families; he'd stand out like a sore thumb. And on that journey I felt so close to those travellers, all bound by a common, humble hope: to live, and to experience pleasure. Such a simple, innocent, raging want.

On the return to London we all watched from the French platform as sniffer dogs checked for bombs under the length of the train. That's the European reality now; *our* reality. And for better or worse we've chosen to remain in it — with no end date.

We didn't know what lay beyond us on that trip. Still don't. What future awaits our family; what land, schools, friends. What peace, what security we can lay claim to. We cling to a London existence, your daddy and I, for our careers, and to satisfy some loose sense of roaming we both have: Australia still feels like it's at the edge of the world rather than the centre. But perhaps an edge is a good place to be. Safer.

'Bali,' Andy repeats.

And that whole experience of Disneyland became unexpectedly moving for us because the place seemed so complete, so sure, in a fragile world where we're striving to make our children's future anchored and secure. They recognised and responded to the certainty of the place and bloomed in it. It was the certainty of childhood, a state of grace before cynicism, fear, doubt. And maybe that's a reason why I'm here in Australia now, with the three of you. I want to give you something of that certainty. You're not meant to grow up thinking traffic light poles could contain bombs, let alone the buses and trains I often take you on.

2 3

Something so vivid on that trip, every trip: the tiredness. Because Andy and I have no family around us to give us a break, ever, no relief. It's a tiredness stretching back as far as our first child's birth, year upon year of it, and it affects every corner of our lives. I need to find some way to be enchanted again, away from the exhaustion. It used to come from striding into the unknown and poetry and the smell of Alice Springs and powering down a road of yelling light and my husband's hips and his laugh and Europe, the dream of it; but I've become too tired. For any of it.

Except, perhaps, home.

Within the thick of the exhaustion there's now often only one enchantment left. Beyond mortgages and tax bills and school fees, beyond the heartbreak of writing, beyond all the uncertainty about where we'll live next and what's ahead there's this one certainty: the joy in you all.

A vivid memory from that trip: Andy chasing after both you boys and scooping one then the other into his arms, holding your little bodies as flat as ironing boards in front of him and singing 'we can fly, we can fly!' while whooshing you around in the bright air. My three Peter Pans; and my chest swelled at the sight. Your daddy and I caught each other's eyes in the delirium of the moment and smiled secrets. We live so much of our lives by reflected happiness now; but in doing so, we have found our own.

Another memory: you three boys chasing each other in giggly circles at the Disneyland gates, and my heart cracking with love as I watched you all. 'Come on,' Andy shouted, but I shook my head. Reality, a writer's reality, had intruded, and I took out my notebook to record another thought, another experience before it had gone from my head; I never stop the working, mulling, jotting. And when I write a change comes over me, a retreating, a disconnection from the world that's almost violent.

On that vast concourse near Paris I took out my notebook and jotted down something I've learned over the years, and that I so often forget. That the most intense happiness is to be found in the simplest of moments: the sight of your father laughing uncontrollably during a film; snuggling on a winter's night into your grandmother's flannelette sheets that have been warmed with an electric blanket; a bedroom filled with the sleep of you children; requited love. And this circle before me of delirious happiness.

I pocketed my notebook, and joined in.

2 4

Henry James wrote of the 'great good place' — that place in your life that you retreat to, again and again, for calm and repose and rest. Most people have one; I certainly do. It's an expanse of water, two hours north of Sydney, called Lake Macquarie.

It's a saltwater lake fed by a channel from the ocean just south of Newcastle, and for years of London living I've dreamed of returning to it. It's about the wondrous circularity of life, a circularity not claustrophobic but healing. I wanted to go back to this slow, sunny place; it represented a pull to home that's deep within — to the simple, burnished happinesses of your own childhood, perhaps — as I aged and had children myself.

I came to the lake a lot when I was young. My grandfather owned a tiny weatherboard boatshed on a rocky bit of land on its western shore, at a place called Fishing Point. Back then the towering gums marched down to the water and the area was sparsely populated with fibro weekenders — simple cottages and boatsheds — mainly owned by coal miners from the nearby Hunter Valley.

My grandfather worked in the mines. He'd lend my family the one-room boffy attached to his boatshed almost every school holiday, and I have such vivid memories of jumping off his jetty and boiling crabs for dinner and fishing with a line wrapped around a piece of cork and playing in the rock pools and larking about in his tin runabout. I can't remember it ever raining or us kids ever fighting, let alone our parents. That place represented pure freedom and happiness, and those simple, sun-splashed holidays have stayed with me all my years.

'This, perhaps, is what it means to love a country: that its shape is also yours, the shape of the way you think and feel and dream. That you can never really leave,' Salman Rushdie wrote.

No, I've never been able to leave it. And now I am coming home. To burnish similar golden memories into the childhoods of my own children, if I can.

2 5

The old roads take me back. It's like returning to a bicycle or a sewing machine after many years of absence — you never forget. All the familiar paths are pulling me north.

'See boysies, that's where we used to stay.' 'That's the lake I swam in.' 'We'd have fish and chips right over there. We'd pull up at the baths in Grandad's old boat, tie it up, and off we'd go.'

'Can we swim in them, Mummy? Can we jump off a jetty? Can we? Can we?'

'You sure can.'

The lake has gentrified. Now it's towering four-wheel drives with windows never opened and a fancy glass restaurant at the Lake Macquarie Art Gallery and Sydney architects doing their thing and expensive boats. But amid all the accoutrements of the new world there's still a weatherboard cottage here and there, tucked away, clinging on tenaciously.

I've managed to find one with the help of my sister-in-law, Trish. A little one-bedroom fibro shack with a red tin roof, nestled among towering gum trees. At a place called Coal Point, near lakeside hamlets with beautiful Aboriginal names like Kilaben Bay and Wangi Wangi, Teralba, Booragul and Awaba. It's tucked in a far corner of the backyard of a couple called Greg and Ilse, who live across the road from the lake, where they've got their own old wooden boatshed and a little tin runabout.

From the minute I see it, it's perfect. Trish, a mum herself, knew exactly what was needed. And deliciously, crucially, it's right next to the boys' school. No more school run, the bane of my London existence. My heart brims at the sight of it all; brims with memory and anticipation; brims with relief that for three months I can just throw you boys over the fence to get you to class. As late as nine am. In my pyjamas if I want.

2 6

Our cottage is simplicity itself and there is such an exhilaration in that. In paring down, shedding skins, leaving so much behind. Gone are the computer games and portable DVD player and toys, so many toys — all the accumulations of our London life that are building over us and stopping us from seeing the sky and the land and stopping us from stilling and taking a breath. I do not want this trip to be a pale shade of our London existence, but something else entirely. A less distracted, less cloistered life. More self-sufficient, closer to the earth. I need it, but more importantly, you kids do.

The American writer Peter Matthiessen said, 'simplicity is the whole secret of well-being' — and you boys are thoroughly modern, busy, twenty-first-century kids. Your life is *not* simple. How on earth will you cope with no web games, no pay TV, no DS? At times the whole idea of this trip feels so experimental and audacious, so ridiculously extreme. Surely I can't drag you children into it.

But the lure …

That endless whining for the electronic gadgets halted, a blessed relief, because you know that all the usual things aren't anywhere in this fibro shack and there's no point in asking for them. The incessant craving for them — the perpetual asking, wheedling, begging; then the complicated process of extricating you from them — depletes me.

When I was young my other grandfather, Pop, used to lock us kids outside the house if we were naughty; he'd tell us to skedaddle, quick smart, and not come back. And while I'd never go that far, there's something about the way of the past — the Aussie past — that's appealing. Get you kids out into the sunshine. Get your little lungs filled up. Toughen you.

It's extraordinary, boys, how quickly your London life slips away in this place, as well as all the clutter attached to it. In a matter of days. If you get the chance to play with electronics at someone else's place you'll seize it all, but in our little cottage you have too many other distractions around you. Such simple things — a long skipping rope, a big backyard with lots of sticks and an old, handmade skateboard, ants on the concrete, a swimming pool, Boogie Boards, Greg and Ilse's dogs, a jetty and the tin runabout that you're soon steering yourselves.

You, Thea, revel in it all. Squeal under the high sky in your bare feet, running far, far from your family into obscure corners of the garden, cackling with glee. You only cry when I scoop you up and bring you inside for a shower. You're filthy, your little feet and knees and hands bruised with grubbiness, but you're zinging with curiosity, energy, *life*. There's sunshine in your soul in this place and I love it.

A sight that plumes me with happiness: you, Thea, collecting shells with Ilse on the shore of the lake and you, Lachie, then you, Ollie, standing with bare feet at the raised bow of the boat as it bumps joyously over the waves, with your arms outstretched and your heads thrown back in the wind and a smile of ecstasy cracking open your little London faces.

I will hold these memories forever, in the fist of my heart.

FROM: NOTEBOOKS
WHAT IS LOVED

The sound of a lawnmower on a lazy Saturday afternoon.

Cycling, wearing an ice-cream carton with eyes stuck on it on the back of your head, because of the magpies.

The dog who'd roll in dead things up bush.

Rain on the tin roof.

The smell of hose water on hot concrete.

Wearing the marks of the sun long on my skin. Bruce Chatwin said he could tell a person was Australian simply by looking at their skin. Oh yes. I can pick an Aussie in Starbucks in Notting Hill because of that.

Eating meals with a can of Mortein on the table.

Walking down a bush track and the deafening sound of cicadas and then it stops as crisp as an orchestra and you'd wonder why, and how.

The clear, stained-glass window of a cicada's wing.

Sunblock at the beach, the spit of salt in the air, all the heady scents of summer.

A river map of ochre lines on your hand.

A cool breeze through the gum leaves — is there nothing finer?

How can I cup the smell of Alice Springs in the palm of my hand forever? How can I bottle it? Sun and dirt and wind and eucalyptus and yelling light and heat-smacked stone.

28

'The old woman I shall become will be quite different from the woman I am now,' George Sand wrote. 'Another I is beginning.' Indeed.

My grandmothers both live around the lake. Each was married to a coal-mining man and came down to the water from the Hunter Valley. The ninety-nine-year-old, Lexie, has recently moved in with her daughter, my beloved Aunty Kay, who's also on the lake. Lexie smells of my childhood; a scrupulously clean smell of powder in folds and soft sheets.

We talk and talk; I just want to drink her up. Her world that's past. She comes out with new things all the time: how 'up the valley' they used to get hessian sacks from the garage and line the inside of the house's walls with them to keep the place warm in winter and cool in summer, when they'd wet them. How she gave birth to my father in a little four-room house at Kearsley that they built with their own hands. There was no pain relief. All she had was a sheet tied to the bedposts to clutch. How she'd 'blue' the clothes to get them white. How she'd put acid in the mix when she'd make her gramma pies — I'm still trying to get to the bottom of that one. ('Probably kept her young inside,' giggles a friend. 'Perhaps it's the secret to her long life.')

Lexie tells me she can make a salad sing. She calls a scourer a 'scratcher' and home movies 'walkie-talkie photos'. She describes someone as 'silly as a wet hen' and says, with a raucous hoot, 'After the mayor comes, the dunny cart comes, always, never forget that.' I could listen to her all day; I walk away from visits filled up.

It's good for you children to see your mother so relaxed, not shouty and stressed and swamped by her London life, which feels so often like I'm swimming frantically to barely stay afloat. A new Mummy is unfolding here at the lake, a more even, serene, quiet one, a Mummy who's uncurling — and laughing a lot.

The rhythm of my writing is changing, too. In London I'm always trying to find wily ways to separate from all of you, to find some restorative pocket of me-time. It's difficult, and it carries a burden of guilt: these precious moments I've snatched for myself are moments when I should be with someone else. Yet I have to write. I feel like I'm living spiritually when I'm working; absorbed, focused, lit. When I can't glean the space to sit at my laptop I feel fretful, lost. And often, the gruelling nature of London living works counter to me finding this serenity, and the time.

For you see, in the thick of the city I can only write when I'm viciously, savagely alone, and motherhood doesn't allow very much of that. 'The centre of our story is the tension between the yearning to create a home and the urge to get out of it,' wrote the American writer Gail Collins. Ah yes — her story, my story, the female story.

At Lake Macquarie our world is simpler, easier. I'm in the energy and rhythm of you children and not myself, for the first time in my life, and it feels wonderful. Intensely creative. I'm rising early with you — not stuffing the pillow over my head and groaning for an extra five minutes, an extra half-hour — and I'm tumbling into bed soon after I put the last of you to sleep. During the day I feel so energised, writing strong in any moments I can and feeling sated when I come to the end of it; not agitated that I haven't done enough, that I've never done enough.

Years ago, in the thick of the baby-swamping, a painter friend in Alice Springs wrote to me of her new studio, which was 'like living in a white balloon'. I dreamed of that, for so long, dreamed of working within such a space. A room of my own that was spare and pale and quiet. I could write in Alice, in the hum of its silence. I found it also, a long time ago, in Antarctica.

Yet I've learned that as a mother I'm at the coalface of living, and for a writer that's a good place to be. Motherhood didn't turn out to be the professional impediment I expected, for you children have hauled me into life. Joyously. I'm no longer in control — I've had to let go, had to relinquish my own raging, wilful identity as a single woman — but perhaps I'm a better person for it.

'I don't want to underlive,' I wrote in a journal as I left Australia for England. And here I am now, living to bursting with you kids. In a very different life.

Rupture is good, yes. The trick is to keep doing it, again and again.

2 9

I'm learning from my grandmothers. Letting things wash
away, letting them go, not holding on to everything so
tightly. 'Don't worry about every darned thing,' says my
ninety-six-year-old Nanny, Win. 'That's the secret, I think.'

She still lives in her little flat alone. She's just had her
eyebrows tattooed because of the arthritis in her hands, and
looks fabulous. She arrived in Australia from England by
herself, as a Barnados kid, aged eleven. Went into a home
near Perth, was trained for domestic work. She's been in this
country ever since. She's fiercely intelligent and a voracious
consumer of the news — watches all the telecasts from five
pm to eight pm, flicking between the channels. I know never
to call her at that time. She's my reference point for where
the country's at; she knows so much.

We're quickly woven into the daily life of her apartment
block, and I marvel at the boundless exuberance and
patience of the elderly people around us. In London you
children know no one older than their forties, your parents'

83

peers, for that is the strange artificiality of the expats' world we live in. These people around you now, in their eighties and nineties, commune so joyously with you; offering you lollies, leaning down to you, ruffling your hair, asking 'how-you-going-cobber?', exclaiming 'you little ripper!' when they hear of your latest triumphant adventures as Aussie-kids-in-training — a mechanical bull at the Cessnock Rodeo, a 'Roar and Snore' sleepover at Taronga Zoo, feeding a kangaroo at the Australian Reptile Park, a swim from a jetty with a dog, a self-constructed slingshot made from a twig.

My heart brims as I watch you all; you children need people like this to give you the breadth of life — and your heritage. Instantly obsessed by your 'nannies', you develop 'the Nanny dance', which involves running in ecstatic circles and chanting their names.

These elderly people are teaching us all so much. Their decency. Their staunch sense of fair play. Their sense of responsibility: you don't let people down. The ability to let things go because that is the secret of serenity. And their laughter, always laughter. 'The philosophy was to be happy, without making other people unhappy,' Aboriginal elder Doctor William Jonas said of his nanna; and you know, there comes a point in your life when you realise that well, yes, why not, it's as simple as that.

And as I write this now I'm weeping. Because I feel a selfishness often now — the selfishness of denying you children the presence, constantly, of grandparents and cousins, great-grandparents and uncles and aunts; of you missing the wisdom of older people; of not having friends who know your family through the generations.

You see I'm torn, as I have been for as long as I've lived this exile's life. There's the urge to stay close to the hearth yet break free from it at the same time. Your daddy, Melbourne-born, is the avowed Anglophile. What on earth will he make of this new world I've found? He needs his cappuccinos and PG Wodehouse Society, his tie with its impeccable Windsor knot and his snowy shirt cuffs, his *Economist* magazine and private London club, Soho House.

In Lake Macquarie, our existence is so simple. For the first time in my life as a mother. You are all filling your lungs with this hurting sunshine. Getting grubbier than you've ever been in your lives. Tanning gently up. Seeing a different Mummy. Becoming best friends with your cousins: one of my brothers, Mark, and I had little boys at exactly the same time. You're playing *Star Wars* with Jaidy and Nardo in the long grass, Monopoly with their pet cockatiels on your shoulders, endlessly splashing together in Greg and Ilse's pool; marvelling at stick insects and cicadas; collecting tiny plastic toys called Go Gos as well as crabs from the lake; doing swimming lessons with them and judo. Soldering the fierce bonds of mateship, for the rest of your lives.

And you're getting to know your great-grandmothers — those two glorious, fabulously different women — before it's too late. The gift of them.

It's all I want, at this moment, in my life.

3 0

A Lake Macquarie park by the water. You're all running and whooping, using muscles you rarely seem to. In this vast reserve, under its glorious canopy of blue, you again seem louder, brighter, taller than in England's crammed spaces.

So many of the larger green spaces in the London suburb we live in are fenced off, private. Yes, there are the free expanses of Hyde Park and Kensington Gardens, but the beautiful Communal Gardens of Notting Hill and Kensington are reluctant, shut off by forbidding iron fences, and can only be accessed by a handful of people wealthy enough to live around them. In Australia the idea of this kind of communal garden is obscene. It just wouldn't happen here. To shut away the best — and often only within-walking-distance — grass is profoundly undemocratic. In England, it's accepted, normal: no one thinks anything of it. I crave a fairer world.

'Oh for God's sake, just bring the boys home,'

admonishes Jess. 'They need some grass. Proper grass. Not that piddly stuff that office girls sunbake on in midsummer, in their bra tops, in the middle of Covent Garden.' I laugh, knowing exactly what she's talking about. 'And they need to learn words like "wussbag". And "dag". And "ginger".'

'"Ginger"?'

She clucks her tongue in frustration: I've been out of the country too long. 'As in: "Tom's very ginger." You know, tentative, hesitant. They'll definitely be ginger if they stay over there too long.'

England is beginning to claim you, my boys. In new company you are initially shy — your eyes sometimes slide away from adults'; you're not used to that fresh Aussie slap of face to face. In the early weeks I find myself instructing you both on the ways of this new land. 'Aussies look you fair and square in the face. They make eye contact. They instantly smile — big, wide — in friendliness. To everyone and anyone. Like this.' I smile wide and thrust out my hand. 'OK?'

You both learn. Unfold. Smile up.

It's something I found hard to teach in England when all around you were people rebuffing the innate Aussie friendliness. Even worse. You, Lachie, when you were younger, used to run up to kids at London's Princess Diana playground and say, 'Hi, I'm Lachie, wanna play?' and the children would turn away from you without even giving their name; their nannies looked on mute, as if there was something odd about your behaviour.

It used to break my heart. Until the ways of your adopted land start growing over you, too.

3 1

These golden days at Lake Macquarie are veering me closer to some kind of a decision: I want you all growing up in a country where children learn an enriching sense of fellowship — or mateship. A country where you learn an engaging boldness of thinking and doing, where sunshine and fresh food grow kids tall. I want you playing with your cousins in bush you're unafraid of. And I want each of you to understand this country's language, *my* language, and not be embarrassed by it; so that when I say 'you nong' in absolute affection, or call you a 'dingbat' with a laugh, you'll know where I'm coming from.

A newspaper article describes this summer season as the 'sharkiest' ever. New word — among so many new words to absorb (anti-venom, blue-ringed octopus, redback, taipan, dengue, tourniquet to name a few). You've learned to shake out your boots every morning and walk through tall grass with caution. To be careful when picking up a stick: it could be a snake. To watch when you sit on a rock in the heat of the midday sun: something else might be on that rock. To not venture too far out into the surf because of sharks and rips. To walk loudly through the bush so vibrations will scare snakes away.

I repeat often that the odd ant is good for you — it's a losing battle keeping them out of the cereal — and sometimes it feels like we're living on an ants' nest. You experience mozzie bites before you know what the perpetrators look like. Kookaburras are in the gum trees outside and nocturnal possum-thuddings are on the roof and strange scurryings are under the house and white cockatoos snow the ground of a local park and pelicans claim high street-light poles as if the structures were installed for their sole use. And you are all zippy with happiness and amazement at all this nature pressing close.

Quickly, easily barefoot, for much of the time; walking down the street in just swimmers and nothing else — sometimes undies and nothing else. Little torsos firming, hair ragged, hearts wide.

In London your energy was so boxed in, frustrated; everything was so close and crammed; concreted over; you'd been contained indoors for so much of your little lives. In Australia, you've quickened. It's as if you've stepped into bigger selves, the children you were always meant to be. Here you can run and dart and laugh and shout and jump into whatever water is at hand — which you do, wherever you can, with the fabulous greed of a person, denied chocolate his entire life, finally let into a sweet shop.

I can't stop smiling in wonder at it all.

3 2

In weekend Skype conversations with Andy our little London house behind him seems so cluttered, full-to-bursting, cramped. Our dimensions have widened since we've been away. But Andy, God love him, looks ten years younger, as fresh as the day he was married. What have we — I — done to him over the past decade?

He informs us, with a Cheshire-cat grin, that he's just had jellybeans for dinner. You boys go wild with excitement at the concept of Daddy's new life. Andy also informs us he's slept in until noon.

'You'll keep, mate,' I say with a grin. 'You'll keep. Your time will come.'

Every night I flop into bed soon after you kids, the exhaustion pulling me into sleep like an enormous rake dragging through my body. But it's a good tired, a tiredness that comes from sun and wind and hard work and happiness. 'You sound so alive,' says a London friend's e-mail in response to mine. I feel it. And strong. Refreshed.

I miss my Andy achingly, didn't realise it would cut so deep. Want to show him, tell him so much. Keep on bugging him, calling, e-mailing; so much to relay, so many new adventures every day. He calls our London home 'lonely land' now and I always seem to catch him on the mobile when he's in the supermarket buying a meal for one. But I feel like this venture has made the relationship so much more vivid, like a varnisher's hand passing over a painting. We both feel the missing, keenly, and it's done our ten-year marriage the world of good. We're more loving and playful with each other in our conversations, more respectful of each other's needs. He wants us to do this again sometime: he's loving the break. Throwing himself into work; not feeling so torn about the demands of his job encroaching on his home life; sleeping in if he wants; reclaiming, gleefully, the freedoms of the single life.

I can't wait for him to see his sun-basted boys and girl, the shock of the transformation. Children are so resilient and I'd forgotten that. I was worried about the disruptive impact this trip might have on you all; but of course, rupture is so much more traumatic for the adults cemented into their little ways.

Or replenishing. It feels like twelve years of London living has slipped off me, like mud in a shower, in a matter of weeks. It's extraordinary how swiftly my northern hemisphere life has receded, and I feel Aussie again, newly Aussie, refreshed.

Of course, the euphoria won't last forever.

3 3

Everything in our new world is the antithesis of the old: lean, pared down, contained. Although our three-room shack is minute, there's no clutter. No leftovers we can't be bothered eating because we only have a bar fridge and there's no room for anything but essentials. No vast amounts of space to mess up and dot about with piles of things — papers, clothes, toys. No endless cupboards and drawers to fill with unnecessary … stuff.

This new simplicity reminds me of a week in London when our broadband was down. It was so peaceful. I felt old-fashioned, serene, sedate. Something like the way I feel now. Motherhood seeks peace, stillness. This basic little cottage makes me feel like I'm suddenly in control, after so long: calling the shots. Remembering the gypsy woman I once was and living like her, strong. Everything here is containable, managable, in its place. There's no excess.

I don't need a dishwasher; there are fewer dishes to rinse, fewer clothes to run through the washing machine (in London, often, it's several loads a day). My life has become managable again and I am fuelled by that.

Perhaps this trip, in some way, is a reaction to the excessive consumption we've seen for the past decade in Notting Hill. When we arrived it was still largely a suburb of artists and old English money threaded amongst a vivid Caribbean community — all a bit louche and ratty and raffish. But after the film with Julia Roberts and Hugh Grant, well, the bankers moved in.

Suddenly it became a suburb of swimming pools in basements, Burberry jackets on Guy Fawkes effigies at the bonfire nights of communal gardens, Porsche four-wheel drives and Filipina nannies. A suburb of greed and gluttony and showing off. And the wealthier and more privileged the people were, it seemed the more careless they were with others. You always knew, as a mum, it would be the non-working bankers' wives who weren't great at returning calls or e-mails, who cancelled at the last minute or mucked people about; their world seemed so unreliable and flighty and spoilt, so removed from the real world.

I felt … *stained* … by it all. After ten years among it I had to scrub myself clean. I wanted to find decency again: a simpler, kinder, more caring way. I didn't feel in any way that having lots of money made you a better person.

We arrive at Lake Macquarie with three small suitcases between four of us. I rotate three cotton dresses hanging on a hook. Love wearing fewer clothes; feel so free and unencumbered; never learned the secret of layers in London. I wear just one pair of shoes, endlessly; they go with everything I've got. Arm myself socially with a red lipstick, don't need much else. Splash my face with water and add a little soap at night. You boys have a few pairs of shorts and a cossie and some T-shirts, Thea some cotton dresses and a baby rashie and some Bonds singlets; Win's supplied some woollen cardies her friends have knitted. That's about it. It feels so free and easy not having to pile on the layers — the baby stockings, coats, mittens, scarves, beanies — that are a necessity of an English childhood, and that weigh down every morning before school. 'Where's your hat/other glove/raincoat? We're late. Come on, hurry up!' We all feel liberated by this simpler life.

And there's a kookaburra asleep in the gum tree outside my window as I write, and, well, as I'm sitting at this table with my bare feet resting on the chair opposite me, the happiness is pluming through me.

In this age of accumulation, simplicity is the key. Shed skins. Find spareness. Travel light. It's exhilarating. I'm becoming a new woman in this place. Lighter, stiller.

34

WHAT IS LOVED

The fact that Australia's richest man is Frank Lowy, a Hungarian migrant.

Standing with two people at a party. 'Look at us,' declared the man in the middle, proudly. 'Three Australians, and three different accents between us!' Yes. And in Britain I never call myself British, always see myself as an outsider. As do all the Aussies around me. But here, they all declare they're Australian even though none of them were born here.

The sign outside Sydney's St Andrew's Cathedral, the main Anglican church of the city, advertising an 'Asian book service' at four pm.

The Aboriginal guy from Botany Bay we chance upon at the Australian Museum, doing a fabulous show about his ancestry, demonstrating Aboriginal dancing, and playing the didj. He tells the cram of people in front of him that he's from the Wallangang tribe ('just change the a's to o's and see what you get') whose area is Botany Bay and to the south of that — the Illawong. This girl from the 'Gong was enraptured; I had no idea of any of it.

The astonishing Asian kids on 'Australia's Got Talent' — twelve-year-old Jal Joshua from Vietnam, ten-year-old Filipina Chelsea Castillo. The full force of emotion and maturity in their voices. You boys are transfixed; and later watch them on YouTube again and again.

The old geezer on his mobility scooter with what looks like an Italian mate on the back of it, who's clutching his walking stick with one arm. Both of them hooting home from the RSL with huge smiles on their faces.

Aboriginal painter Rover Thomas standing before Rothko's 'Brown, Black on Maroon' at the National Gallery of Art in Canberra in 1990, and reportedly saying: 'Who's that bugger who paints like me?'

The fact that you, Ollie, Thea and Lachie, are descended on your father's side from the family of Captain Cook's botanist,

Joseph Banks, and on your mother's side from two convicts. And that you now have Chilean and Maltese aunties, a Scottish step-grandmother and cousins with Maori and Aboriginal ancestry.

'I can sense the joy or sadness of many places,' Archie Weller said. I've always felt that about Kings Cross. I've lived in two flats in the thick of it now, and it seems to me a place that's soaked in sadness, no matter how vigorous the efforts are to clean it up. Someone once told me there was an Aboriginal massacre there ...

'Don't wait until you die to be free.' Written on the wall outside the Lake Macquarie Art Gallery. From Alma Rachel Skinner (1928–91), a member of the Stolen Generations.

3 5

We had timed our arrival Down Under for the Australia Day weekend and, as we set off from our wintry London home, there were small signifiers along the way of the lovelinesses that lay in wait for us ...

At Heathrow: the bleached blond hair of the young Aussie boys in the boarding queue — the sheer *sweetness* of them. They were checking in their surfboards (gee, they'd been optimistic in this land of muted waves and pebbled beaches).

The naïve friendliness and charm of the old Aussie couple striking up conversations with the people around them; their quiet pride as they chatted about Sydney's weather; their dry, chuckly humour. Yeah, I'm going home, I grinned to myself. And I can't wait.

My mother met us in Hong Kong to help with the last leg of the journey. (Let me just say it was a mistake to have only a three-hour stopover with an eighteen-month-old and two other kids.) When we arrived in Sydney Mum quietly moved to a different queue to have her passport checked. 'Is she embarrassed by you?' asked the customs officer loudly. Mum and I laughed and laughed.

The gladness swelled as I passed two Qantas hosties on their way home from their respective planes, meeting in the wide corridor and having a good old gasbag after what seemed like very long shifts for them both. They looked like they'd been colleagues for years; they were so open and warm and loud, absolutely tickled pink to see each other. It made me miss my own Aussie girlfriends very much. The mateships brewed through childhood and uni and relationships and traumatic break-ups and divorces and children and parents passing on; people who know your vast and complicated history just as you know theirs. Relationships fundamentally different from those fresh, intense friendships of the expat life. These ones are deeper, older, richer — so cherished — because they've endured through so much. Silence and distance the most. One from kindergarten, several from primary school, many from high school and uni and work; and we pick up where we've left off, like I haven't been away, like it's hardly been years since I've seen them, and I love that so much.

As I walked the streets over those first few days what struck me was the looseness and optimism and innocence of Australians after the cynicism and world-weariness of Europe; their disarming, fresh friendliness; it all seemed so bright and bubbly and insecure, like teenagers growing too tall, too fast.

How quickly you're subsumed into this new, shiny world; how quickly everything else — terrorism, startling economic woes, Europe's gas pipeline being shut down — seemed so very far away. In Australia the excitement seemed to revolve around the start of the television ratings season. The biting recession of grey, weary, battered old England seemed a world away. A friend I thought I knew well exclaimed over an old newspaper she'd randomly picked up in a Bondi café: 'Did Benazir Bhutto get assassinated?' It was an anniversary piece; it had happened more than a year before.

This is the Australia Andy dreads, and I know exactly where he's coming from. 'Just go back there and switch on the Channel Ten news — that'll make you never want to live in the country again,' he's been teasing for the past decade.

36

On Australia Day itself we're at Bronte Beach with some mates. I stare in fascination at the young adults gathering for their drinking and dancing and barbecues. The flags draped around their shoulders like capes, or painted on their cheeks; the southern cross tattoos on a shoulder or a calf; the balconies draped in the flag; the Aussie-themed hats and towels.

Where did it all come from? What's happened over the past decade? And why are the police watching them so intently, I ask. 'Because of Cronulla, the riots.' I see. But it all seems innocent enough, and I'm struck by the sense of unembarrassed pride these kids have; how alien it all seems compared with my own Australian youth.

Over the next few days another picture entirely emerges: the ugly side of nationalism that I thought only the likes of Britain had with its football hooligans rampaging across Europe a decade ago. On Sydney's Manly Beach, young adults have 'FUCK OFF WE'RE FULL' painted across their torsos; up and down the coast there are people draped in the flag spitting at Australians from other backgrounds; some were jumping on cars, smashing windscreens, yelling abuse, threatening and posturing. 'WE GREW HERE YOU FLEW HERE' read some of the banners.

It was utterly shocking, utterly dispiriting. What's happened to my country? It's not an Australia I can be proud of in any way. It's a nationalism I've missed entirely, one that's risen in the past decade, fuelled by bleakly divisive legislation and a crude need, I guess, to reassert a strident and ugly identity in the wake of the Bali bombings and 9/11. It feels so juvenile. Like a harking back to the stultifyingly narrow, dispiriting, stifling 1950s. Suddenly, another Australia entirely was presenting itself.

I flinched in response. The euphoria of return dimmed; the golden bubble of loveliness I'd been existing in had finally burst.

37

It's almost as if Paul Keating's dynamic attempts to change the flag and create a republic in the 1990s rocked the boat too soon, too fast; led to a rattling of national identity that opened up a chasm of resentment from which has sprung this crude, volatile jingoism. Those poor, deluded kids. They have no idea. It's so reactionary, unthinking, mindless.

It also reminded me of what I love about London, why I get that heart lift every time I walk through its Soho streets. Because it feels that yes, all of life *is* there, and it's tolerated, feels fabulous and free and dynamic. Embracing. Grown up. Of course Britain has its problems with political parties like the far-right, openly racist BNP (British National Party) and its *Daily Mail* grumblings about too-many-immigrants from Eastern Europe; but London, in particular, feels a step ahead.

It's why I love a city that has a plethora of newspapers and the *Spectator* magazine as well as the *New Statesman* and *Private Eye* and talks and debates from authors and academics almost every night, somewhere in the city, and the engine room of a deeply intelligent BBC 4 that is the world's best in the medium and is listened to by a huge percentage of the available audience; and a myriad of kids from all manner of countries around my children as they're growing up, so that when Obama was elected you boys had absolutely no idea what all the fuss was about his colour. You just didn't get it — why wouldn't he become president? He has a lovely smile, that's why he won, isn't it, Mummy? Because you don't see colour, or difference, the way older generations do. That is the beauty of London. It feels like the future. The only way the future can work. A future I'd like my kids growing up in.

A short while after Australia Day this little gem is also reported: a young bloke in board shorts, with bare top, bare feet and wearing zinc cream, is crossing Bondi's iconic Campbell Parade. A message is painted on the surfboard under his arm: 'Save Bondi, Free Ivan Milat' (in reference to all the foreign backpackers at Bondi). Not even remotely funny. Just … dispiriting. It's the side of Australia the Brits do not like.

The newspapers are rightly horrified, at all of it. Sydney's *Daily Telegraph* has this message in response to the specific ugliness of Australia Day: 'Don't get so shitfaced that you smash bottles on zebra crossings that kids will walk over, don't take over the kiddie rock pools with your drunken parties …' Quite. It's not the spirit that made Australia great, and it's not the country I want my children growing up in.

This is.

The Australian of the Year, Mick Dodson, calls for a new Australia Day, not associated with 26 January, which for Aboriginal Australia is Invasion Day. Fair point. It's quickly shot down in many quarters, but it's raised an interesting issue. This response comes in, also in the *Daily Telegraph*, from a man only known as 'David': 'This man is a true patriot. He wants to change the name of this day and have Australia Day at another time. This means another public holiday — what a champion.'

I laughed out loud; the best Aussies always make me laugh out loud. It's why I'm married to one. And why I want to bring him home.

38

The dry, vividly Aussie humour amid an ecomonic downturn: an old XF Falcon by the roadside in Wyuna, country Victoria, with a sign that read 'For Sale — Four Slabs'.

'I'm going back to negotiate to see if he'll take slabs of light,' said the bloke who alerted the Herald Sun.

The tyrannical station leader at an Aussie base in Antarctica who wasn't giving the summerers (people who stay at an Australian scientific base over summer) their quota of grog. So just before they left, on the last ship out before winter, they buried a huge stash of toilet paper in the snow.

'I use my husband's toothbrush on the dog' — an anonymous guilty secret on the back page of the Sydney Morning Herald.

The dog named 'Victim' because it was hit by a car.

The reptile wrangler at the Australian Reptile Park telling the assembled tourists around him — Aussies, Americans, Japanese, Germans — about his time as a teacher at nearby Wyong High. 'I left because I asked the class, "What comes at the end of a sentence?" "An appeal."' The Aussies laughed the loudest.

The Marrickville Anzac Club, sold to a developer after going into voluntary administration. The stories, the legends. The local cop who passed out drunk under the table and woke with one of his eyebrows shaved off. The time a doorman wouldn't let one of the regular's dogs in, so he stamped a paw in the sign-in book. The time another cop handcuffed the supervisor to the table because he didn't want to go home.

An entire coastal town in New South Wales, called Hat Head, which had been forced to queue at forty-four portable toilets after the region's sewerage system failed. Big smiles on the faces of the Maynard family, pictured outside a Portaloo and carrying a roll of loo paper. Everyone in good spirits. 'The jokes haven't started yet but I'm sure they will come,' said one resident.

39

A December fifteen years ago. What felt, then, like the perfect Christmas. I was living in Alice Springs and had fallen in with a group of scientists. They'd discovered a waterhole west of the town that very few white people knew about. On Christmas Eve we loaded up the four-wheel drives with swags and bush ovens and tins of tea and tinsel for the anointed pine. We were all without family — childless and Godless. The land was our cathedral. And none of us wished for anything else.

Bush tracks faltered to the secret destination, they lost their will and almost petered out. When we arrived after several bone-jolting hours we selected the appropriate pine for its trussing with all the solemnity of ceremony. Then we climbed a rocky bluff and drank margaritas under a magnificent sunset that seemed as wide as heaven itself. Our bush Christmas had begun and it would last for several days. We felt cool and exclusive, modern and defiant.

It was a blessed world away from all the ghosts of Christmas past. Childhood ceremonies of tepid turkeys with too many family members crammed into airless, sweltering lounge rooms. And after divorce fractured everything — the complication of allegiances. Travelling from gathering to gathering, to aging relatives from opposing factions who hugged you too tight and cooed identical 'my haven't you grown's. And these were people who were once great friends but never spoke to each other any more — as a child it was all too bewildering. As I grew older the split-family shunting and sweltering lounge rooms never changed, but the questions did: 'Have you got a boyfriend yet?' 'When are we going to get grandchildren?' 'Are you happy, love?'

A magnificently selfish, secret waterhole near Alice Springs was heaven compared with all that. Out bush, happiness flooded me. Friends were the new family and wasn't this the way of the modern world? I'd chosen this lot. Like-minded people. Cloistered by our shared desire to be Elsewhere. We were all from somewhere far away and all relieved to be removed, to some extent, from the various hooks of family obligation. Presents home had been sent weeks ago. We were now free and alone and it was bliss.

Well, that was then.

40

One of the signs of passing youth is the birth of a sense of fellowship with other human beings as we take our place among them.

Virginia Woolf

Another December. London. Standing beside you wide-eyed children at a Christmas-carol singalong in the fabulously excessive gold and red exuberance of the Royal Albert Hall. Belting out all the familiar carols from childhood — *Away in a Manger, Silent Night, We Three Kings.* And something is catching at my heart as I stand here, led in song by a twinkly Santa. The wonder at the pull of all this. At the twists and turns of life. The way I've slipped into living within the world, rather than alongside it.

I sang a lot of these songs thirty-five-odd years ago, as an angel wearing a sheet at Keiraville Public School in Wollongong. And here I am now, singing them all over again. And the happiness is so intense that if I could step aside from my body I think it'd just burst into light.

All these childhood carols are resonating like the first pop tunes — the songs from childhood and teenage years that still tug when you hear them. (*Throw Your Arms Around Me*, *Wuthering Heights*, *Carol of the Birds*, *O Come All Ye Faithful*: the heart-lurch, basically, is the same.) And I know that I'm now embedding these Christmas carols into your own psyches, so that as adults, when you come to hear again the lullaby-loveliness of so many of them, you'll feel an emotional pull too. A tug back to a time of happiness and security and wonder and enwrapping love, before everything gets chipped at by adult uncertainties. These carols for me are invested with layers of meaning and it's not exclusively religious; it's to do with something deep within a person's emotional core — whether you believe in a God or not.

4 1

What happened when I had you kids?

As an adult I'd never done church — it was for people in strange places like Cooranbong where Lindy Chamberlain lived. I worked at triple j, read *Rolling Stone*, went to the Sydney Film Festival, dressed rather too often in black turtlenecks. God don't figure in that world.

Yet occasionally, once a year or so, I'd find a church service somewhere and just ... sit. Usually in some foreign place where I was an anonymous backpacker and none of this embarrassing behaviour would filter back home. But there was something ... *all-calming* ... about these occasional illicit experiences. A little leak through the veneer of aspirant coolness; a gentle drip through my deeply restless, anxious, often bleakly-alone twenties. I felt 'righted' in some way by these secret Sunday assignations. Balmed.

After those tumultuous twenties I arrived in London with a backpack, a manuscript of a novel and a vague plan to shift gear. Life up to that point had been so greedy, busy, grasping — there was little time for stillness. Andy, your daddy, had invited me to share the Fleet Street bedsit. We were both doing night shifts to pay our way in our deeply expensive new country. It was an exhausting, freezing time; it felt as if the chill had curled up in my bones.

Andy sensed I needed something else in our new land — an anchor — and one day he took me to St Bride's across the road (it's known as the writers' church because of its Fleet Street location). It has a beautiful Evensong service every Sunday and I found myself slipping into regularly going. It was like meditation. After each hectic week I was brought down into stillness by a spiritual enveloping from a service mostly sung. I felt calmed, lit. Those evenings were clean, the shining hours.

We eventually climbed out of our one-room existence and churchgoing slipped away. But then we had you children, and something tugged within. I found giving birth a profoundly spiritual experience — the pinnacle of joy as a human being — a time when I was thanking God, a lot. And there was an urge to find a kinder, gentler, stiller existence. For myself, and you children.

I don't think it's surprising that I experienced this tug as a mother. There was a desire to find a little more grace in this greedy, addled world, and the older I get the more I respect words like grace, and empathy, and kindness. Words that experience a little surge at Christmas, like an ocean swell of loveliness.

A lot of the time I don't believe. I say no, it's ridiculous, I'm with the Alice scientists on this one. But then sometimes I'll find myself standing alone at night, in the bedroom quiet with the sleep of you children, just … breathing you in. And then a great warmth floods through me — an enormous, glittery, heart-swelling gratitude — and I find myself closing my eyes in unstoppable thanks. Prayer is gratitude, oh yes.

42

The world softens at Christmas time. I never sensed it during those Alice Springs days but I do now. It's not just the longest public holiday of the year. It's a celebration of love — for those closest to us and also, more generally, our fellow human beings.

For example: a London car park. Three pm. The sky glooming down. Running late, and cold. Grumpy? Oh yes. A Muslim man was walking toward me. He looked deeply religious; he was bearded and robed. I'd just read that Al Qaeda was possibly planning a Christmas terror campaign, focusing on people travelling home throughout Europe for the festive season. Let's just say I wasn't feeling particularly … *open* … at this moment. My whole being was one huge flinch. There may even have been a scowl.

'Would you like my parking ticket?'

'Pardon?' I said.

'I've got two hours left on my ticket and I'm going now. Please. Have it.'

Well, stun me with kindness. I looked right into his face, properly this time. Saw not a Muslim but a fellow human being beaming nothing but compassion and friendliness and generosity. *A light heart.* I couldn't say thank you enough; the smile I gave that good man stayed on my face deep into the night.

Christmas is a time of cracking open hearts, for all of us. I love it for that. The world undergoes a surge of meaning and over the years that meaning may change but it's meaning nonetheless. What it is to be human. To be good, to hold out a hand. In forgiveness. Gratitude. Love.

43

Later in that December of the Muslim parking ticket. The London Library. Cosy in an old leather armchair as the dark crowded into the day outside. Reading a copy of *Meanjin*, the Rock and Roll issue. The scrawled, original lyrics to the Triffids' *Wide Open Road*.

> *The sky was big and empty*
> *but my chest filled to explode*
> *I yelled my insides out at the sun*
> *yeah at the wide open road.*

Suddenly there's a catch in my heart. For who I once was — that funny, fierce Alice Springs girl — and for home. The world that I've lost. Yelling roads. Its light.

You see, that London Christmas was to be busy and noisy and lovely for Andy and me, with a gaggle of Aussie-expat orphans around us, as usual — but actually, I was ready again for those crammed family Christmases in sweltering lounge rooms. I'd come full circle.

I recognised, finally, that family — not the individual — is the basic unit of society. Do we all realise that at some point? That year my brother was hosting a Christmas lunch at his home near Sydney, with his boys who are the same age as my own, and he'd invited my mother, and both our grandmothers — who have rekindled their friendship.

I wanted to be there.

I wanted, deep in my core, to go home. I wanted you children to have the richness of cousins on tap as well as uncles and aunts. Grandparents. *Great*-grandparents.

I also wanted to find stillness, somewhere, on Christmas Day. Because in the stillness is something wondrous. England is still largely silent for this one day of the year — you can't even get a tube to Heathrow. It's like the world pauses for a moment, holds its breath. And if you let it, if you can find it, the silence leaks into your soul.

When I look at a Rothko painting at the Tate Modern it feels like stillness and love and wonder and loneliness and beauty all at once — something deeply human and deeply mysterious, spirit-brimmed. And those qualities, to me, are encapsulated in Christmas. The season is a concentration of all the things that give me solace in this life — beauty, silence, generosity, merriment, stillness, singing, love. And maybe faith is nothing more than wonder at profound mystery and beauty — the wonder in a Rothko painting, or a Bach composition, or a ticket proffered, with a gentle smile, in a London car park.

PART THREE

44

We wove a web in childhood, a web of
sunny air

Charlotte Brontë

Once it was squealing through sprinklers on a sweltering
summer day and running around Hills Hoists in tent
tunnels and never calling grown-ups by their first name.
Once it was knowing all the kids in your street and darting
in and out of each other's houses like fish and Mum feeding
anyone who was around at tea time. Once it was Dad
shooing you outside and expecting you to disappear for as
long as possible. Playing on building sites. Dogs never on
leads. Six and out cricket on the road. Once it was feeling
unencumbered, free, safe.

An Aussie childhood. The one so many of us remember.

Mothers old at thirty-six. Ten showbags from the Easter
Show. Footy cards on the spokes of your bike. Slapping a
tennis ball in a stocking onto a wall behind you. The corner
shop for mixed lollies and maybe a packet of ciggies for
Mum. World Book encyclopaedias but brainy houses had

Encyclopaedia Britannica. Cream buns at the tuckshop. Tying shoelaces. Mum curled over the sewing machine. Sugar sprinkled on lettuce to make you eat it. Being taken to the airport to watch the planes. Sunday roasts at your nanny's; she put bicarb soda in the veggies to 'colour them up'.

Pretending to smoke fag lollies. Sunny Boy triangles. Fairy bread and chocolate crackles. Milo sandwiches, chip sandwiches, tomato-sauce sandwiches. Vegemite and butter worms from two Vita-Weats squeezed together. Mini banana lollies, bullets, freckles.

The good old Aussie cake shop with fly-ribbons of plastic on the door. Cream buns and lamingtons and ice-cream birthday cakes. Chasing the Mr Whippy van down the street as it played *Greensleeves*. Fish and chips and potato scallops wrapped in newspaper by the beach. Feeding the chips to the seagulls. A big family celebration? Chinese at the local RSL.

Scissors paper rock. Elastics. Skipping. Drawing all over the driveway with chalk. Sliding down grassy slopes on cardboard boxes. A cool shower to take the sting out of sunburn. Peeling the flakes of skin off your shoulders. Ant farms and totem tennis, yo-yos and jacks. Riding the inner tubes of tractor tyres in pools. White foam surfboards.

Cracker nights with Tom Thumbs and Ball Shooters and Bangers. The drive-in, and pretending to be asleep on the way home so Dad would have to carry you into bed. Bob-a-Job at Brownies and Cubs that took you into the homes of strangers. Having to dress up for Sunday School. The ABC *Sing!* Book. Going to the tip with Dad. Putt Putt Golf. Competitions with your siblings to see whose Easter Eggs would last the longest.

Chinese burns. Brandings. Flicking a towel across a friend's bum. Water fights with a hose. Stacking twenty cent coins on your forearm and catching them. Billy carts and slingshots. Trail bikes and slug guns.

Clag glue. Project books. Compass sets. The kid who'd eat the Perkins paste (there was always one of them). Desert boots, Dunlop Volleys and Bata Scouts with compasses in the heels. School milk in glass bottles that had been warmed by the sun. Dressing paper dolls in paper clothes with tags. Malvern Star bicycles. Roller skates with thick rubber wheels.

Brown paper bags from the grocery shop — no handles. The haberdashery shop for material. Sleeping in the back of the station wagon — no seatbelts, but lots of blankets and pillows and the moon following you. Riding your bike in the street, no helmet.

The smell of rain on a newly mown lawn. Swinging around and around the Hills Hoist in undies over a sprinkler until the clothesline sagged. Being told to get outside and play; to skedaddle, scat. Mud dams in the gutter. Collecting tadpoles in jars. Yabbying in the creek.

To find something of all this is why I've brought you children back to my country. I have little idea if any of it is left. I'm an Aussie-mum-in-training on this trip.

45

And now? Well. We all learn fast. The Aussie childhood could possibly involve talking to 'G'('*Puh-lease,* "granny" sounds far too aging.') on her Skype video link — that was the realm of science fiction, *Star Trek,* as I was growing up. Might involve a grandmother taking the kids to Baby Proms at the Opera House or the Christmas Wiggles concert or a local café for a babyccino. She might put on a Harry Potter talking book in the car and, if the kids are lucky enough to get a trip to the Easter Show, it's usually one showbag now, or two at a pinch — they're so expensive, and let's not talk about getting in to the place.

Mum? Probably working. She doesn't have a sewing machine any more — what's the point when Chinese clothes are so cheap and all the kids want are labels anyway? Banana smoothies are a snack and slurpies and microwave popcorn a treat and sometimes it's a takeaway barbecued chicken for dinner, or even cereal; Mum's so tired, she never stops running about.

It's all rice crackers and noodles now, Thai and sushi. And to tempt kids in the supermarket there are King-Sized Mars Bars and Jumbo-Sized Samboy chips — Australia, shamefully, now has one of the highest childhood obesity rates in the world.

Today, there might well be more vehicles in the family than parents. City kids listen to Mum abusing other people in her car — school runs are best for this. It's not surprising if she's in her forties or fifties and it's hard to get volunteers for the tuckshop any more let alone school reading programmes, but good old Aussie mum — she's still changing that *Sesame Street* song from Zee to Zed.

She no longer sends the kids down to the corner shop for a banana Paddle Pop as a reward; she's got the ice-creams in her freezer. And she's not too keen on them walking to the shops by themselves anyway — there might be a paedophile or God forbid another mum in a four-wheel drive on a mobile phone.

Kids' parties? Rarely at home now. Who entertains in their house any more? Who needs the stress and the mess? There are all the allergies to deal with and you might have to label everyone's drink with their name so no one gets germs and every layer in pass-the-parcel has to have a gift so every child wins, everyone's sense of worth is preserved — and don't the boys seem to have bigger energy now? (Could it be because their little lives are so relatively sedentary?)

The guests might each take home a personalised gift that could well have cost more than the present bought for the birthday child. Indoor play centres are popular, also Build-a-Bear or beauty or fairy parties, or celebrations not only with live entertainment but live animals, or VIP extravaganzas complete with red carpet and disco. Now, of course, it's all about being famous for being famous — celeb heiresses and reality TV 'stars'.

A playground ditty: 'Paparazzi in my hair, paparazzi everywhere.' But the Ginger Meggs spirit lives on — the classics are still being gleefully bludgeoned. Current among certain six-year-olds: 'Waltzing Matilda, everybody killed her. Lying on the grass, with nothing up her arse.' And 'Joy to the world, the teacher's dead, we barbecued her head. And what we did with the body, we flushed it down the potty, and round and round it goes, and round and round it goes …'

I giggled when I first heard these, but dread you boys ever taking them back to your London school. The teachers there would be horrified; they wouldn't get the larrikin spirit that never fails to crack me up. The fabulous, cheeky Aussie irreverence that's Bunty in *Seven Little Australians*, Paul Keating putting his arm around the queen, Hoges, Dawn Fraser, Graham Kennedy, CJ Dennis.

46

The typical Aussie dad, God love him, isn't so great with the toolbox any more. Loves watching *The Simpsons* with the kids. Was there at the birth but shudders at the thought of the business end. A treat is taking the tin lids to Maccas (it's also the number one spot for weekend custody exchanges).

A girlfriend reports few fathers at her local Montessori on Father's Day. The same nursery also has a noticeable quota of same-sex parents. Another friend has lots of adopted kids at her son's school — from China, Thailand, India — and a fair few IVF twin sets.

School classes could be combined and called 3/4 Latte. It's so much more multicultural, international, cultural now. Aussie kids go to the art gallery more often and their school might even have an artist-in-residence along with a wormery and bush-tucker garden. In the playground it's not so much cops 'n' robbers but *Star Wars* light-sabre fighting. They check out the ABC website, play Mathletics against other schools, learn PowerPoint and website design. They hand in assignments on disc, researched online.

Their world comes through the computer screen. Once it was don't go near anything electronic or you'll get the strap — now we rely on kids to show us how the damned things work. (And the naughty ones are no longer required to stand in an empty garbage bin in the school playground — discipline might involve the 'reflection room' to think things through.)

Child minders? Often, too often, DVDs and laptops. It's a little breather for Mum and Dad but God we feel guilty about it. Kids read a computer screen more than a book. Find clips on YouTube, love Facebook and Playstation, iPods, Nintendo Wii and texting. Teenage boys used to talk about how powerful their car was — now it's their computer.

A lot of kids stay indoors, cocooned safely in their bedrooms, in absolute control of their world. Is it any wonder? Parents preach distrust and wariness and caution. Outside are paedophiles and kidnappers and bullies. Aussie children aren't marinated in nature so much now, grubby and stinky-hot like they used to be, sun-basted and sweaty and lean-limbed.

Kids don't talk to strangers. Aren't able to trust the man who asks if they'd like to see his puppy. They have awareness now; will attempt to fight potential abductors off. They don't stand to offer their seat as much to pregnant or older people (you three need to learn this so it becomes second nature: how to help your grandmothers, just be with them, it's part of the great circle of life).

Aussie kids aren't left at home alone as much any more; parents don't quite trust them, either. If they have to run down to the supermarket children come with them and, instead of latch-key kids, there are after-school clubs. In the old days, children were given more confidence to feel safe. When are they allowed to cross the street by themselves now — as opposed to when we were kids?

No more running barefoot: there might be glass or needles.

No more organic play: visits to parks or friends are organised and supervised.

No more basking in the sun: it's continually battled with No Hat No Play and rashies and 30+. The only people who are sunburned now are the tourists (ahem).

And water restrictions have killed off that simple, euphoric Aussie-summer ritual of swinging around the Hills Hoist in your undies over the sprinkler. I can't find a sprinkler any more. Let alone, in a new Aussie house, a Hills Hoist. Or an expanse of grass. Professor Tony Hall of Griffith University says the good old Aussie backyard has largely disappeared from freshly built suburban homes. Windows are becoming smaller, and once-treasured natural light and labour-intensive gardens and lawns have made way for double garages. People have started building homes they think others will buy, and the new designs often imply — dispiritingly for our kids — an entirely indoors life.

4 7

Aussie families don't necessarily know their neighbours any more and might not want to. Parents are far too busy rushing around, getting the kids from after-school activities and rushing them straight indoors, increasingly through their double garage so there's little contact with the outside world.

Children are protected in friendship circles. They have scheduled playdates, mobiles from primary and it's always known where they are. They're *over*protected. Their world is child-centred. Parents are at their beck and call; kids expect to be entertained. They call grown-ups by their first names and when they visit someone's house they just open the fridge and ask for something — or worse, take.

Adults in return are hovery, paranoid, demanding, competitive. Buzzwords: 'helicopter parenting', 'Bubble-Wrapped kids', 'ADHD', 'overscheduling', 'G and T' (who are the Gifted and Talented/getting tutoring/seeing a child psychologist). There's speech therapy and cosmetic dentistry and Kumon and Boxercise and sports training and swimming squad. Anti-bullying strategies are big; there are courses on bouncing back from adversity; kids know their rights but not, necessarily, their responsibilities. There's more confidence now: with talking to adults, expressing opinions, demanding attention.

A mate who's a teacher says it's harder to discipline. 'There's an assumed … familiarity,' she shudders. Kids answer back. Don't automatically accept an adult's word ('But why, Miss?'). May well tell the teacher to fuck off. Know a lot more about sex than we did. Specialist sex educators come into the schools. 'They're teenagers at ten,' laments a friend with older children.

Is it all too grim? My sister-in-law, Trish, described you boys as 'like something out of Narnia' when she visited us in London a year or so ago. I think she was implying some extreme kind of innocence perhaps, but Australia, I suspect, has shaken it out of you.

'Joy to the world, the teacher's dead, we barbecued her head …'

48

Yet, yet … I'm spooked, and heartened, by things uncannily similar to my own childhood.

Elastics still, and scissors paper rock. Chocolate crackles and Dunlop Volleys (retro groovy). Skateboards. Choctops. Ant farms. Miss Mary Mac. Skipping ('teddy bear teddy bear turn around, teddy bear teddy bear touch the ground'). Siblings still have competitions to see who can make their Easter Eggs (or Easter Bilbies) last the longest. *Behind the News* and *Play School* are still on the ABC.

Brandings and trampolines. Pink Zinc. Totem Tennis. Bindis and mozzie bites. Footy cards collected and traded. Roadside stalls — though instead of homemade lemonade they might be offering massages. Sliding down grassy slopes on cardboard and random sightings, still, of chalked hopscotch on footpaths.

All around me are parents trying, like me, to etch golden childhood memories of their own into their kids' lives. One mate knits with her son, another does papier-mâché, another sold up in suburbia for a block in the bush with chooks and a veggie patch and horses over the back fence. A friend's eleven-year-old daughter landed a paper round but her parents drive her and her mate there and then watch over them as they complete the job.

I ordered *The Brady Bunch* series on DVD but you boys were bored: you wanted something else. Television was edited more languidly then; children can't concentrate like they used to. Your world's so fast, zippily edited, everything's a sound bite or the length of a YouTube clip. My teacher mate says kids need to be taught in smaller timeframes now, six minutes at the most before their attention wanders.

All the parental despair, anxiety, guilt. That we parents are catapulting our kids into adulthood too soon, pushing too hard, cramming their worlds, not giving them space to merely … be. A kid. Bored. Lonely. Still. Not allowing enough spontaneity into their lives. Not letting them just laze on the grass and watch cloud animals in the sky, not letting them sit on a cubby-house roof and make up adventure stories, just explore and discover and potter and bask in all the glorious wonder of childhood.

I'm guilty of all of that, and I'm trying to redress it with this trip.

49

Is it all too bleak?

Ali Clunies-Ross is the daughter of an old school mate. She's thirteen and she e-mails me her Sydney world. Alongside MySpace, Facebook and texting she lists: 'going to the movies on a Saturday afternoon, skipping on the school terrace, lemonade stalls, sliding in the mud when it rains on the school fields in your sports uniform, singing on a bus on the way home from an excursion, heading straight to the beach after school when the holidays start.'

There's a catch in my heart at her words, my eyes prickle up — because of that feeling of being vividly, burstingly alive that I remember so clearly from my own childhood. You kids are a lot younger than Ali but after her e-mail I thought, well, there's hope for you all yet.

The surfing journalist Nick Carroll conveyed a similar feeling when describing his younger brother, the world champion surfer, as a child. 'Tom will probably just laugh at this or maybe kill me because of it, but probably my fondest memory of him was when he would have been three years old. I remember him running through our house, just wearing a singlet and underpants, squealing with delight. I had the same kind of childlike delight in being alive, an unchannelled kind of feeling. And there's something magical about that. I sometimes wonder whether we've both been trying to get back to that with our surfing over the years.'

That euphoric delight in just being alive. That's one of the reasons I've brought you kids to Lake Macquarie; to cultivate it; to have the sight of it ravish my heart.

And you know what, I see that delight in you boys as you charge home from school for your iceblocks and run down to the water for a spin in the boat and grab the Boogie Boards for a dip in the pool and jump squealing off the jetty with your arms outstretched. And I see it in you, little Thea, running away into the far corners of the garden, giggling madly at the 'wow-lers' (flowers) and prancing on your chubby little legs that I just want to eat. All of it, all, intoxicates me with joy. And there's not an electronic gadget in sight.

Then this came in from a friend, Mary Regan, who's raising her ten-year-old son, Louis, in Sydney's Kings Cross.

'We were walking home from school through the Cross and Louis asked, "Do you like it here?" I replied, "Well, it's kind of scuzzy. Do *you* like it?"

'"I love everything about it," he said.

'Then he told me of the flower baskets hanging from the poles and the people and the lights that shine in the trees at night that "look so elegant". I was in awe of his beautiful vision of his neighbourhood and felt relieved and humbled.'

The joy and rapture are still there. Kids will always find them. Maybe they're just hard for us, as adults, to see. I used to think that parents had to teach their children to wake up — to the wonder of the world, its beauty — but perhaps, of course, it's the other way around.

They teach us so much.

PART FOUR

5 0

When you boys register for your new school, Coal Point Public, on the shore of Lake Macquarie, you are barefoot. After we've signed you in you're still barefoot as you wander through the aisles of Woolworths with me, behind three barefoot little Nipper girls skipping along in their cossies and caps, their dad in tow.

I love this country for that. An English friend reeled back in horror when I tried to go barefoot, once, in the streets of Notting Hill. 'Eugh, that's so dirty.' There, perhaps, yes. In Australia it feels like childhood; it feels free.

'Where are the mountains?' you, Ollie, had exclaimed when you first saw your new school. Because the Australia of your imagination is tall and wild and broad and wide. Well, you may not have mountains but you have an Aboriginal bush-tucker garden at the school's entrance, huge playing fields fringed by the bush (top field and middle field), a big, well-stocked library and an IT lab with twenty-eight computers.

You are both wide-eyed; you've experienced nothing like this in London. You go to a private school there and are both taught in the same (temporary) demountable cabin that's subdivided into two classrooms. Your playground is the local public park across the road. You, Lachie, have access to six computers in your classroom; you, Ollie, have three; and there's no library (although it's planned). It's a great traditional education, focusing on the Three Rs, but we're not getting much in the way of facilities. That's London, and we accept it, and pay for it. Suddenly, though, I'm not sure why.

Coal Point is a typical-looking, semi-rural Aussie primary with weatherboard classrooms and wide wooden verandahs and asphalt. Near the entrance are large aspirational signs: 'Public Education: Our students are Australia's Future', and 'Achieving for Students, the Community and Australia'. Stirring slogans that lift everyone higher: the teachers, students, parents, the wider community. The sense of pride in the nation's young — that these children are to be nurtured for the good of the country — is something that seems obvious but is never made apparent in the UK. Of course, it's British reticence, but it's also something they'd never think of doing. It's a different way, a different philosophy over there, not nearly as inclusive or bolstering or positive. The hard, bright light of Australia complements this optimism. England's light seems too milky, diffuse, is resolutely not optimistic.

In the UK the state education system often feels like it's failing, and Andy and I, as parents, have been caught up in the fear of that. That's why we've chosen to pay for a private school. But I had a wonderful state primary education myself, in Wollongong, and I'm fascinated to see what happens when my little Londoners enter this one.

5 1

I'm worried about you boys being bullied because of your English accents. 'You just take a step forward and tell them to rack off, then they'll want to be your mate,' instructed your uncle, Mark, several days before you started school, and you both solemnly nodded and took note.

'What's rack off, Mummy?' you, Ollie, later ask.

Ah yes, a whole raft of new words to absorb. Nick off, wagging, bludging, dobbing, chucking a sickie, swimming carnival, library bag, tuck shop. (Oh, the endless delight of that last one. Particularly when Andy hears I'm actually going to be a tuck-shop mum for the first time in my life. He gleefully files his order from London: 'pikelets, cream bun, Anzac biscuits, flavoured milk, Vegemite sandwich'. In fact, when I finally come to do my bit, you, Ollie, the Brit, are the only one in the entire school to place an order for that last item on the list.)

On your first day, after six hours of motherly anxiety, both of you boys burst out of your classrooms, joyous.

Slipping into your new Aussie lives like knives through soft butter, and once again I'm in awe of the resilience, and adaptability, of kids. It's the parents who berate themselves with the guilt and angst; the kids just do it. 'Your accent's awesome,' a classmate had told you, Lachie, on that very first day, and from then on I knew you'd both be fine.

Why do you love your new school so much? 'Because the teachers walk around with microphones at playtime, Mummy, just like *The X-Factor*!'

Well, I actually think the principal may have a lot to do with it. Kim Creswell (Ms Cressy, as the kids call her — it'd never happen in the UK) came from a tiny town called Urbenville, near Lismore, in northern New South Wales. And lived in — you guessed it — Urben Street. Her previous school had thirty pupils in total ranging from kindergarten to year six. She's hungry for her charges to succeed — and to be happy. To me, she represents the best of state education in this country:

'The love, passion and excitement of my life has been to watch the eyes, sparks and smiles of students,' she wrote to me. 'To observe the "penny drop" moment. The pride of success.

'As a public school educator in Australia for seventeen years, I've had the absolute pleasure of being a part of so many lives and assisting in the creation of futures. I've proudly stood in front of many classrooms as a teacher and for the last five years as a principal, with the belief that if students know you love and care for them, the learning simply happens. If children feel safe, happy and comfortable in their classroom and school, everything else just works.

'Innovation, enthusiasm and adaptability are the attitudes I aim for. I want to — as Gary Marx, the educational speaker would say — "create a sense of positive restlessness that encourages everyone to think and learn about how we can constantly be better".

'Our beautiful school by the lake is extremely privileged to have outstanding students and a wonderfully supportive community. Most importantly, we have exceptional teachers. They provide our students with the opportunities and environment to be the amazing, creative thinkers our world needs. As a school leader, my personal motto is: "Expect the best and you will get it. Expect nothing, you get nothing." It sums up how we should feel toward students, staff, parents, school, learning and life.'

I couldn't wish for a better school and, after paying for the privilege in London, I couldn't wish for a better education than the one you boys are getting here, in this tiny place on the edge of the Hunter Valley, at this time in your lives. You would lose nothing by being in the Australian education system permanently as opposed to the English — and would gain something, I think.

52

'The amazing, creative thinkers our world needs.'

That's what the headmistress of Coal Point Public aspires to nurture; I cannot say the schools in London have that same audacious, yet simple, sense of breadth and ambition. This woman is not pigeonholing in any way; is not saying you can't, don't even think about it; she's telling everyone — students and staff — to take on the world and be the best they can. I had it instilled in me as a child and, as the days turn into weeks at Coal Point, I know that I want you children to have it instilled in you, too.

That phrase, 'being the best you can be', crops up again and again while we're in Australia. There's nothing embarrassing about aiming for it; it's natural competition, and it produces the Obamas and Rudds of the world. In England it's more opaque. It often feels like 'ambition' is a dirty word. Any encouragement 'to be the best' is shied away from; in the school system everyone's a winner; no one knows their place in the class; school reports aren't graded; we don't want to boast; you have to be humble and meek, muddle through in the British way. I have an English friend who is horrified by the phrase, horrified that her children would be exposed to such a system. But she's upper middle class and she's had a very good education herself and a privileged life; she's never had to fight for what she wants.

I prefer the Australian way. I'm a coal miner's daughter who was the first in my family to finish school, let alone make it to university. If you work hard enough, you can get through. The system will support you and applaud you. I ended up with a scholarship to a rigorous and expensive fee-paying Sydney high school. I still feel that in England you can get through if your parents are wealthy enough to afford the astronomical school fees of private education; that gears you to entering the next elite stage of education then the next. I prefer a more level playing field; something fairer.

And as I stand under the central sun shade of Coal Point Public at 3.05 pm, waiting for all the big-boned, bright-eyed Aussie children to spill out of their classrooms, the little London children we've left behind seem so delicate and pale in comparison. Worried over, fretted over more, compared with these large-spirited, chatty, vivacious Aussie kids. I'm guilty of hovering, as a London mum, and in Australia I'm letting go.

(And Aussie kids really do seem so big in comparison with their northern counterparts. Research shows that babies are taller if their mothers have a large dose of sunshine in the last three months of pregnancy — and here, in this place, it shows.)

You boys are becoming so much more grown-up over here, self-sufficient, stronger, freer; running off to school by yourselves and coming home by yourselves, sometimes even letting yourselves into the cottage and getting your own snack; dressing yourselves, cleaning up after yourselves. 'It's the Australian way,' I keep on saying to you both, and you're buying it. As a mother it's a huge relief. I'm finally learning to step back a little, and you kids are flying.

Something is happening in Australia: you are becoming the children I always wanted you to be.

5 3

Every afternoon you boys run home bursting with news of your days:

Three Lachlans in Lachie's class, when in England they often can't pronounce the name (Lash-lan, Laysh-lan). 'Who are Captain Cook's pirates, Mummy?' (Because this new person you're learning about is a captain, like Jack Sparrow in *Pirates of the Caribbean*, so he *must* have pirates attached to him.) 'I want to be in the Premier's Reading Challenge!' 'There's a school disco!' 'I'm doing a convict diary, I've got to pretend to be a convict.' 'We're doing Mathletics, it's the most amazing thing,' (a computer program pitting together kids of similar ability in mathematical contests, worldwide now, and developed by a Sydney school teacher). 'Mummy, Mummy, the school choir is going to sing at the Sydney Opera House; can I audition?' That uplifting sense of reach! That 'yes we can' mentality as opposed to an 'oh no, we couldn't possibly', 'we must stay in our place' kind of world.

The Australian system allows kids to be kids at a more leisurely pace. In England they must start school, by law, at four; you, Ollie, by dint of your birth date, would have started school eighteen months later in Australia (and you were so desperately young when I packed you off, heartbroken, in your London uniform, barely beyond your toddler years).

It all seems so crammed and accelerated in London: more narrowly focused on the traditions of writing and reading. In Coal Point there's more space around learning for other activities (sport, art, etc) and it also feels like it's much more embracing of the wider world — with its emphasis on computers and interactive teaching — despite the tyranny of distance.

This primary education system, on the edge of the earth, feels far more dynamic — more *in* the world — than the one you kids have left behind in London.

5 4

Every afternoon you run home to Paddle Pops in the freezer because I'm an Aussie mum now and I've learnt fast. Then it's early to bed, often with no protest. We're all knackered, but it's a good healthy tiredness from hard work and fresh air. And so begins our lovely, easy Lake Macquarie rhythm.

I don't think I could do this, with such intensity of joy, in Sydney or Melbourne. They're too much like London: too harried; each just another city. Couldn't bear to negotiate clogged urban roads to get you to school every day, in no way would it feel like a break from our regular life. As soon as I drive into Sydney I can feel the aggression and frustration; people closing off.

At Coal Point I can feel myself unfurl; in this fresh lake air, among the tall gums; there are our possums on the roof and our curious white cockatoos and our kookaburras telling us whenever it's going to rain. I couldn't claim this simplicity in an urban space. Have to be close to the earth for it to work. Have a craving for nature that is intensifying as I age; the comfort of it; as my London life gets more stretched and swamped and stressed.

You children need to know this land, my land — perhaps yours eventually. 'If we do not have our land, our children will not know who they are,' Hal Wootten QC said once, quoting an Aboriginal person. It's important for any child, anywhere; they need the anchor of it.

You don't get much of the land in London, the sense of the bones of the country and its great heart and its soul. It's too built up. There are rivers that once traversed where we have lived, tributaries of the Thames that have long been covered over (the Fleet, the Westbourne). Australians are distinguished by their connection to the land; there's so much of it around them; so much of it still in its virgin state. And I'm trying to encourage you children to dive in to it because you're incredibly lucky to have it so accessibly close. You can so easily feel the pulse of the land; in England it's much harder — it's so built up.

As I get older I realise there's really only one aim in life: to wring the most happiness that we can out of our time here on earth. The wonder increases as I age, at all of it: this whole intensely beautiful, surprising, ravishing, maddening world. And as I get older there's a clarity, the great upward curve of it: simplicity is everything.

5 5

There's such a firming with these days at the lake. A spare rhythm that feels vital right now for my serenity, and my writing. I wake just before seven to a giggly tumble of you kids running in from the bedroom for a cuddle on my single bed that's tucked into a corner of the living room (you, Lachie, always lift Thea from her travel cot; in fact, she's started calling you 'datty' on this trip). You boys then turn on the telly and watch your cartoons while I organise school lunches and breakfast. It's usually Nutri-Grain, which we can't get enough of in Australia. (It's almost five pounds a box at our *chi chi* 'Grocer on Elgin' in Notting Hill, and I only treat us in London when a royalty cheque comes in. The lot is usually gone in a day — in fact, we've been known to have several bowls of it for dinner on the day of purchase.)

You boys dressed and scrubbed up, you're champing at the bit to be off. You dash outside and stand on a high verandah of Greg and Ilse's to watch the teachers arriving (we're next to their carpark that's threaded with gum trees), then as soon as it's 8.45 you're running, literally, to school, so eager; and I can't help laughing at it. And chuckling that I'm not going with you — liberated from the fumey, infuriating school run, at last!

You, Thea, and I then drive ten minutes to Toronto for the day's supplies; the papers, food, nappies. A drive that's relaxing for its wide streets and sparseness and winding, ever-changing view of the lake. Some days it's on to the grandmothers for a cuppa (Nanny Win seems to have an endless supply of nurses and cleaners and friends helping in her tiny flat, as well as her daughter-in-law; there's always someone calling in and I'm so grateful for that.) I'm back at my writing desk by mid or late morning; you, Thea, are occupied next to me by a box of Duplo borrowed from a mum down the road, or the saucepans and strainers from the kitchen cupboards (I twist rubber bands across the handles of the ones I don't want you getting into). You sleep for several hours after lunch, and that's when I really get cracking with work.

At three, everything's put aside for you boys barging home, often with your cousins; or you'll go to my sister-in-law's for playdates. If we're at our place we'll most likely be by the pool, then it's an early tea and early to bed. Myself included; and all my exhaustion is gone. As is the woman I'm ashamed of, with the voice I don't like.

Only once did this world go awry. You boys were splashing about in the late afternoon; I was on a sun lounger, the laptop propped in front of me. You, Thea, were playing with some toys near us all, in your absorbed, self-sufficient way. You had your red shoes on, which you adore; stupidly I thought this would mean you would never want them wet.

In an instant you were in the water. Silently. I remember looking up and catching your wondrous face as you sank, down, down, your little arms outstretched. I was straight in after you, clothes, cherished watch and all. My thudding heart. Still thudding, even now, as I write this. The speed of it. The silence. You loved the big adventure (another cause for concern); the big tumbly wet then Mummy's clutching cuddle and the endless holding and kissing, so tight, afterwards, like I'd never let you go; the enormous fuss with you at the centre of it.

I never had my laptop by the pool again.

Was reluctant to tell Andy, felt like such a failure as a parent, but the boys blurted it out instantly on Skype. He understood, thank God; yet it was a chilling lesson. And perversely, it's made you, Thea, fascinated with the water; from that point on you just wanted to get into it. And have your mother soaked from head to foot, I'm sure, all over again; you thought that was hysterical: Mummy dripping wet.

The worst of times, but it's the only heart-thudding incident we experience at the lake. The rest of it is such a glowing sojourn in our lives. Mum driving up from Sydney to stay for several days at a time, my girlfriend Donna flying down from Queensland; visiting my aunty for chinwags and Uncle Bruce's legendary carrot cake; Dad popping over for cuppas and lunches of fresh bread rolls filled with barbecued chicken from the supermarket (the latter surprisingly hard to get in London). And when I let slip about Thea's little adventure, it's fascinating the yarns I'm told in return. I saved my younger cousin Robbie once when I was eleven, in a very similar situation, and had completely forgotten; all around me are tales of near-misses involving pools.

Such a quintessentially Aussie story, and one you rarely come across in England. Most London kids around you boys don't even know how to swim; in Australia, you're way behind your peers in terms of ability. And you've been learning since you were four. You Thea, too, will be starting lessons; quick smart.

PART FIVE

5 6

Horizons feel constrained in England. Where is that bold and vibrant imperial race that conquered the world? The country seems to be populated by a pale, clammy set who look like they've never had a decent vegetable in their lives, can't get near a dentist, cough a lot and have never been told to cover their mouths. 'England is a backwater. Let's be frank. The trouble with England is that it leads the world in nothing but decline,' its pilloried literary son Martin Amis wrote. A country still obsessed by Empire and all that it lost, agitated by memories of glories past.

A disappointment has crept through my years in England. Am I disillusioned because the nation — that glorious, distant, all-knowing, all-conquering Motherland of my childhood — let me down? I couldn't find very much of the London of my imagination when I arrived. The city felt meek, cowed, yet curiously aggressive: cracking and groaning under the weight of its age and population. It absorbed resignation. A lot of London didn't look like it was supposed to look (unlike Paris, or Venice, or New York). You saw pockets of the imagined land — the buildings swelling out over Regent Street like the chests of puffed lions, the sweeps of Mary Poppins terraces in Mayfair and Regents Park, the gold and red drum of the Royal Albert Hall — but there wasn't so much of it left.

'To the English ... Americans are a sort of mutant breed, whose optimism is a sure sign of emotional aberration,' the English theatre critic, John Lahr, wrote in the *New Yorker*. 'The English are constitutionally unable to fathom it, and for good reason. American optimism has its roots in abundance and in the vastness of the land ... Britain, on the other hand, is an island the size of Utah. Its culture is one of scarcity; its preferred idiom is irony — a language of limits.'

The longer I'm in Australia, the more it becomes apparent: I'm ready for the muscularity of another way of life.

5 7

FROM: NOTEBOOKS

'There's a label on some English mineral water — only the Poms could write this sort of bullshit — that said "gently carbonated". Well one thing I hope I am never is "gently carbonated". Paul Keating, post-PM.

Reading of the couple who'd died because they didn't want to disturb their doctor. They had pneumonia. So English, so reticent.

Martha Gellhorn, on why she loved England: 'For its absolute indifference. I can go away, spend six months in the jungle, come back and walk into a room, and people won't ask a single question about where I've been or what I've been doing.'

Catching this snippet from a Frenchwoman talking on a Radio 4 programme about her time in Britain: 'I can never get used to the lack of feeling. Especially with the men. No one looks at you on the tube. Men don't look at women, people don't touch. It's like a no-man's-land.'

Tom Stoppard: 'Where did the English acquire this curious reluctance to engage with one another?'

Joseph Fiennes, on a drama teacher: 'He must have been a Canadian or something. He was just too warm and generous to be British.'

The writer Adam Gopnik on Charles Darwin: 'He was an extremely English Englishman, with an Englishman's desire never to sound like a know-it-all, coupled with an Englishman's conviction that he alone knows it all.'

Jeremy Paxman: 'The English assumed that somehow all other races were just aspirant English men and women.'

King George V: 'I don't like abroad. I've been there.'

58

'Londoners have been forced to sacrifice the best qualities of human nature,' Friedrich Engels wrote of Victorian London; it often feels like that's still the case.

Something has happened to me in London: I don't like people. Or at least, not very many. It makes me want a very specific, tucked-away life, removed from most of them. They get into my head and clatter about in there, sapping my serenity; stop me from working and finding a replenishing stillness. They're *everywhere*.

And I don't like the woman I'm turning into. There's no longer enough of a smile in my voice. Sometimes I can't be bothered looking people fair and square in the eyes any more; sometimes I'm a little too curt. England makes me turn away from people; Australia makes me laugh with them. And my God I need the tonic of that.

In London, enthusiasm feels like weakness. The four treasured English girlfriends I have found in the UK all have the gift of it and, interestingly, each is an outsider in some way: Jewish, or Scottish, or restlessly from the countryside.

Several years go I met an Israeli journalist in a Notting Hill café and he was so warm, vital, curious, full of life. It was such a shock: I'd forgotten people like that. I felt myself becoming sparkier, looser, lighter in response, remembering a woman I once was. A stronger, flirtier woman than this cowed one. It decided me: I'd been in London too long. I'd become less vivid over the London years and hadn't noticed. I think it's something to do with the sun, a straightening of the spine.

I feel like the energy between England and me is wrong. My new country has stolen my optimism, and I had such a lot of it once.

59

There's a trigger for this pull to home. The plunge into simplicity. The desire to live a different life.

Last year, Andy lost his job. And we lead what looks like a sparkly London life but it's an illusion: we have no savings. Every month every penny is spent on kids and a mortgage and we have nothing left until the next blessed pay packet arrives. It's a ridiculous way to live and suddenly, in one afternoon, our fragile house of cards came crashing down.

Andy was given one month's salary. He'd left a secure position he'd been in for six years for a new adventure, but a month after he arrived the woman who'd lured him there left for a better job, leaving her man high and dry.

One month's salary. With a greedy monster of a mortgage. And we were due to renew it and with Britain plunging deep into recession it would be impossible to get a new deal with the only stable breadwinner unemployed. I bring in money as a novelist but it's not regular enough to sustain our family of five for a long stretch of time. And more importantly, the bank managers wouldn't be convinced: my income is too inconsistent.

We had to act fast. Inform our mortgage broker. Put the house on the market. Give notice at your school. We were faced with the Big R. Repossession. Losing the family house from under us. God, those first few nights: shattered by uncertainty, sleepless, harangued by the horror. Everything upended, a migraine like an axe embedded in my right eye.

That headache lasted three days. Of holding it together, of phone calls to families and school and a handful of beloved English friends who reacted in the gloriously heart-lifting way I knew they would. One offered to pay your school fees, another begged us to take her country cottage. That was the only time I wept: broken, finally, by kindness.

But there weren't many friends I felt comfortable informing and it was a fascinating sorting process: a fair few I couldn't bear to tell, yet, because even though we socialise there's something competitive about our relationship and I couldn't face the searing humiliation, the delight dancing behind their concern, their almost-smiles as they absorbed our misfortune and rushed off to tell others.

Then something extraordinary happened. As Andy and I split open our lives to fate — wherever it led us — I felt a great weight lifting from me. An incredible lightness of being; almost an exhilaration. That the years in London of living on the edge, of money worries and keeping up with the Joneses would all, suddenly, evaporate. And ahead: the gift of a simpler, lighter life. One that wasn't held hostage to the monthly bank statement.

Suddenly, I felt stronger than I had for years. Free. Released. Creative. Surging with adrenaline, determined to keep the happiness flowing. How did bankers steal the world from everyone else? What happened to creativity and ingenuity, compassion and kindness? Why was greed the quality now celebrated?

It was a cleansing time for Andy and me. We talked — deeply, honestly. We have three shining, healthy kids and it's all that matters and happiness doesn't depend on a flash new car or a kitchen renovation. We didn't need all that stuff around us.

Start afresh! Remember how we lived as students!

With this sudden lightness came the courage to tell everyone. And all around us, so much sympathy and honesty and warmth, so many people living like us, murmuring things like 'there but for the grace of God go we'. I had misjudged the situation entirely. I realised that we live differently from our parent's generation: *these things happen*. There's not the stigma there once was. If we had to lose our house, well, we'd just put up the fairy lights somewhere else.

Then another upending turn of events: Andy got another job, much better than his previous one. But it was a bittersweet relief, because I'd grown to love that brief window of freedom and opportunity that opened for us, that chance to *shed*.

Now to this. Barely six months later. Four of us in a one-bedroom fibro shack, with Daddy to join us at the end of it. Still wanting to hold on to that tantalising dream of lightness, of shedding, of release — even as the money came back.

A postscript. My mum, who'd been staying with us in Notting Hill during all the drama, flew back to Sydney the day Andy got a new job.

'Do you want me to change the sheets?' she asked.

'No, leave them,' I said, and smiled, and that night I curled up in the bed she'd slept in, still stamped with her smell, and deeply slept. For one night I needed the security of childhood, that time long ago when parents didn't live like this.

60

The final visit to my local London supermarket before I leave for Australia. A man and I arrive at the checkout queue at exactly the same time; he cuts in ahead of me, without looking at me. For his entire transaction he does not engage once with the Indian woman behind the till, make eye contact with her, say please or thank you.

Ready for the tonic of another way, oh yes.

London is being chipped in the head with the tine of an umbrella, and it drawing blood, and the woman not stopping, not even looking, as if I am the fool for being in her way.

Why do English people never say what they mean? I've learned that 'Would you like another cup of tea?' means 'Could you go now, please?'

175

A country where 'What paper do you take?' is a personal question bordering on impertinence.

They say sorry, for everything, in a meaningless way, and I've started saying it too. 'Don't say sorry unless you've done something wrong,' admonishes the chatty checkout chick, laughing, at my local Lake Macquarie Woollies (as I lean on the fruit scale, yakking away, then pull back). Of course, she's right. Thea drops a drinking cup at Bronte Beach and a man stoops to pick it up. 'Sorry,' I say in response. 'Why are you apologising?' he asks in bewilderment. Yes of course, why indeed? 'Thanks.' I smile strong.

Often the first response from an Englishman to an Australian: irritation. 'Not another one,' said my editor when I first joined the BBC's World Service. And there wasn't any joking in his voice.

In those early days I'd meet new colleagues and say, 'Hi, I'm Nikki,' and they wouldn't respond with their own name; would leave me dangling. It was huge shock at the time. Now I'm used to it.

'There are still many fastidious Englishmen who, whenever they hear an Australian vowel sound — from a nanny perhaps, or an archbishop — are forced to agree with Angela

Thirkell — an entire continent peopled by the lower orders.'
Stuart Reid, in England's Sunday Telegraph.

'Unlike us, (Australians) don't make an instant assessment of
everyone they meet, based on speech, dress, accent and
general appearance. It takes us a few seconds and we do it
instinctively.' Columnist Simon Hoggart.

Not the only race, of course, to feel the chill of English
condescension. 'She hated the heated houses and lousy
plumbing less then the snobbery and crushing putdowns,' Al
Alvarez wrote on Sylvia Plath's Cambridge days. I've often
thought that yes, a London winter, in bleakest, chilliest
February, would be an apt time to commit suicide. I can
understand why that month, of all England's months, would
have dug its claws into her.

61

An abiding memory of our early days in London: Andy asking me, in the depth of our first northern winter, to warm my fingers on a hot water bottle before I touched his skin. That's how cold we were in our little one-roomed flat.

And then summer, so tentative in this rain-soaked land. By late July I'm urging the sky, 'Come on, get a grip.' And every year there's the sinking feeling come the August long weekend, at the end of the month, that marks the official end of the British summer. Because the season, often, has barely begun. Last year August was overcast for the entire month. Not a single day of blue sky.

On and on roll the soft, wet days. Until that day of clenching cold, usually around mid-November, when the winter nestles in for several long months. 'Gloomsday', it's dubbed. Oh yes.

I feel only a little alive in the depths of a British winter. Flinched by the cold and the dark, wanting to lie under my duvet and sleep away the season, sleep away life for a couple of months.

'Do you know, I believe we should all behave quite differently if we lived in a warm, sunny climate all the time — we wouldn't be so withdrawn and shy and diffident,' speculated Trevor Howard's Alec Harvey in Noël Coward's quintessentially British film, *Brief Encounter*.

After years of living in England, I behave quite differently when I'm away from it. The country is closing over me.

6 2

So, to that vexed question of return. How to respond to the mantra from parents, grandparents, siblings and friends — 'When are you coming home?' It's a dilemma for so many of us expats, which is sharpened by brief visits back where we're confronted by the shock of the aging in older relatives; by nephews and nieces we've never met and friends who've disappeared into a different, settled, domestic world. The insistent query about homecoming is extremely difficult for a lot of us to answer. 'I want to, I really do, but not yet,' is the best a lot of us can do.

Unlike many of those Australians who fled their country in anger and frustration in the 1950s and 1960s the current generation often doesn't have that burning desire to put Australia behind them once and for all. We travel to enrich our lives, but a lot of us now aim to bring that experience home at some point. But when?

A friend in his mid-thirties, who's lived in London for fifteen years, said that wherever he spends his fortieth birthday will be where he spends the rest of his life. Yet the restlessness that's been tugging at my skirt since my early twenties is still with me, and haunts me now: the greed of it. It's a restlessness that's forever luring me on, willing me to find fresh landscapes. But I'm a mother now and that's changed everything.

My craving at this point is overwhelmingly physical: to be locked in the sunshine. Myself, and my family. It makes me young again, strong; the cold makes me shrunken and old. In deepest winter the light in England begins losing its vividness at quarter to three in the afternoon and you can feel the greed of the gathering dark. The night rounds in on us, and the cold, for several months.

I've learned to wear colour in Britain, the brighter the better. For I know that if I wear my usual black in the depths of those London winters I will drown in it. And in the frosty mornings, when the days begin so reluctantly, dragged from the long nights, I dream of moving from this congested island into the light. For in those winters my body is goose-bumped under the snivelly shower, the bits of me not hit by the wet. And when spring comes it is often not sunshine, but mere brightness in the sky.

'Today it was just a dry leaf that told me I should live for love,' the poet Gerald Stern wrote. Well, to paraphrase: today it was a wet, black leaf that told me I should live for Australia.

6 3

Yet, yet, yet, I cherish the great addled zoom of Britain. Despite everything have grown to love this dynamic, shifting, weather-obsessed city. Its fractious, enveloping, scraggly energy; the glorious hugeness and variety of it. It's so creative, invigorating, dense. The art galleries with all those paintings that in Australia you only ever see in books; the theatre that's the greatest in the world; the deeply eccentric libraries; the dazzlingly beautiful shops that have everything you could ever desire. The sheer *confidence* of it all. It so often feels like the world's best. And I have a chuckly affection for the ridiculous, competitive relationship between my two countries; the motherland and the cheeky upstart that's never quite reverent enough. English people often look surprised when I say I'm loving it in their land — but I am.

London has always been a red city, sanguine, with all the energy that entails. It's a place you can go to lose yourself and start all over again: reinvent yourself. I came to England full of dreams, expectation blazing under my skin.

Auden equated loneliness with freedom and yes, there's the quintessential loneliness of the outsider in being an expat. But to be free is also to be enriched, humbled, exhilarated, enchanted, challenged — all of those things I've experienced in London.

Why are so many of us Aussies lured so strongly by the siren song of Elsewhere? To step away from the narrow, judgemental, often suburban little worlds we know so well, where everyone goes to the same school and university; gets a job in the same locality and never moves beyond a radius of twenty kilometres. I left for London when I was thirty to take a detour from the highway of the probable and the predictable, a road that wasn't clearly signposted, and I wasn't too sure how long I'd be travelling — or when I'd come home.

Few Aussies find the expat's journey a smooth ride, but most recognise the gifts that come with being severed from your comfort zone. Some talk of the freedoms of anonymity, of being a different person from the one they are back home: looser, more relaxed, less in control — and more tolerant when things go wrong. Some talk of the greater understanding they have of Australia when it's viewed from a distance, in a world context. For many, the whole tone of their living has been toughened, grubbied: but gloriously so. They revel in it.

And many of us revel in London. I certainly have. The myth of the city isn't a containable one; there are so many

Londons, from so many ages; and isn't that all part of its dynamism? I love playing in history in this place. Love that my locality has blue plaques on its houses stating that writers as diverse as Thomas Hardy, James Joyce, Ford Madox Ford, Agatha Christie, Katherine Mansfield and George Orwell all lived there at some point. Love that down the road is the Royal Geographical Society, whose iconic lecture theatre has hosted not only Charles Darwin but Ernest Shackleton and Edmund Hillary.

'Energy is eternal delight,' William Blake said, and I feel that of London itself. While I'm staying at Lake Macquarie Andy sends me care packages of magazines from various British newspapers and they all seem so energetic and buzzy and loud and creative — all that diversity of opinion, and all that tolerance of it.

'Part of my evil plan!' Andy scrawls gleefully on a card he slips in with them. To lure me back to Blighty for good; to seduce me afresh.

A question mark between us indeed, and I no longer know how it can be answered.

64

To my favourite building in the world. In London's St James Square, behind Piccadilly. It houses a communal room dedicated to the most viciously solitary of pursuits — writing. A place monk-like in the concentration of its inhabitants, each person absorbed into a world barely a metre square, a tiny microcosm strewn with notebooks and index cards and laptops and towers of books from which entire worlds eventually emerge, each wondrously different from the other. So to my beloved hive of writers, where no one speaks, and I am addicted to it. It is the London Library.

The addiction began twelve years ago. I couldn't write in the tiny Fleet Street room. The space was dark and cramped, I had to open my windows too wide to feel the day and twist my head to catch the sky. There was the relentless distraction of the phone and the kettle. And there was Andy. The ex-boyfriend I had joined in London as part of a bold experiment. 'God, your life's a mess, come to London and start afresh,' were the words he used to lure me across.

And so I did. Several months in he informed me, somewhat distressed, that I typed like I was wearing boxing gloves. That jackhammers on the building site nearby had nothing on me. That it was a little *traumatic* to witness the ferocity in my hands. And so for my birthday I received a gift subscription for a year, or, as he put it: relief.

The library rescued the relationship. It also gave me some of my dearest friends. For I was deeply lonely in the flinty city until I found the magical building on St James Square, the London of my imagination. You see, no one may speak in the library's writing rooms — but then there's lunch. And after a rousing session on titles and deals and contracts and poverty and yet more poverty (except for the screenwriters among us but we don't hold it against them), it's back to the writing room, to be balmed once again.

It's a place to breathe out in the city of fractious energy. The library stills me, gives me serenity and calm and focus, similar to the feeling I get after a lengthy swim or an occasional visit to a choral evensong.

65

The extraordinary thing is that you always seem to get lost.

Frances Partridge, a Library member for seventy years

I still get lost in the London Library, still love getting lost. The building arrests time, drags you into its rich, dark depths and holds you there, captive, absorbed, distracted. It's difficult to just 'pop in' for five minutes; there are always delightful diversions and rambles that stretch into chapters and twice now an entire book in one golden day.

I met Andy there once. Waited in the entrance hall for half an hour before he appeared, slightly dishevelled, with a thin accumulation of dust from the shelves he'd been trying to extricate himself from. 'Sorry, got lost in philology,' he explained, and until that day neither of us knew what the term meant. Now, 'getting lost in philology,' has become a catchphrase between us, meaning 'to lose one's way, for some time, in an unfamiliar but deeply endearing place'.

> The sheer extent of the collection
> staggered me. I have always had an
> obsession about books, and in this place I
> felt like a sex maniac in the middle of a
> harem.
>
> Colin Wilson

God the place is sexy. Even the smell of it: that intoxicating scent of paper and leather, of printed words, waiting. And deeply eccentric. It's the only library I know that doesn't subscribe to the Dewey Decimal system. Once I had to do some research on sex, and asked the then assistant librarian, Christopher Phipps, if there were any books on the subject that might be of help.

'Oh yes,' he replied enthusiastically. 'You'll find them in Science and Miscellany, under two subjects. P for pleasure.' A pause. 'And F for flagellation.'

'I'll take pleasure,' I replied.

> It is not typically English, it is typically
> civilised.
>
> EM Forster

That sense of civilisation is epitomised by the glorious reading room, joyous with light from its tall windows. A room hushed with cerebration, thick with an atmosphere of scholarship — or sleep. I've seen a beautifully dressed, elderly gentleman place a white linen handkerchief on a leather seat before taking a very long time to lower himself into it. I've seen a large man asleep, head thrown back, mouth agape, hands crossed protectively over a book on his chest like a dead man's bible placed by a widow. There is a deep, deep peace to the place.

The writer John Wells interviewed a library assistant about the room: 'Miss Bolton … tiptoed about, approaching Hilaire Belloc when he talked too loudly with a printed notice saying "silence is requested", and regularly patrolling the armchairs by the fire on winter afternoons, giving the back of the chair a jolt if the snores were disturbing other members. Her most touching memory is of one lady who always used to come in and sit on the floor by the fire and rest her head against a gentleman's knees. I don't think they ever spoke.' There's a novel in those last two lines.

I do not believe that there is another library of this size which contains so many of the books which I might want, and so few of the books which I cannot imagine anyone wanting.

TS Eliot

I have borrowed *A Portrait of a Lady* and *My Brilliant Career*, both, of course, first editions. I have a habit of dog-earing pages but try not to with library books, mindful of the value of the volumes I'm handling and the gift of trust bequeathed to me as a member. A legendary assistant librarian from early last century, called Mr Cox, apparently waylaid a young lender who had brought back a dog-eared book. Mr Cox shouted at him, 'Right, you wait here!' He then heaved himself off his high stool and returned with a stack of books, all of them with pages turned down. They were banged on the desk with a roar. 'I've been looking for the culprit for some time!'

Mr Cox particularly enjoyed humiliating
any writers he did not approve of, asking
JB Priestley, as he lent forward to sign a
book out, to repeat his name more loudly.
He did so with great embarrassment.
    'Priestley!'
    Cox gave him a fishy stare, and asked,
'Initial?'
John Wells

I've read about a communal place for writers in San Francisco called the Writers' Grotto, a loft space with cubicles. They're entered by plastic accordion doors. There's a punching bag and spontaneous rounds of office golf. It all seems so very far removed from the writing spaces of the London Library, which I think I can safely assume will never be introducing office golf.

To me, the building's like a long cool drink after a sweltering day. It has anchored me to London for almost the entire time I have been there, and is a reason that the city is so very hard to leave. I can't quite describe the peculiar little skip of joy inside me whenever I walk through the library's front door, but I get it every time.

66

One quintessentially British ritual I love is the Proms, the series of summer concerts at London's Royal Albert Hall that collects the best musicians from around the world and sells shockingly cheap tickets to the masses, if they're prepared to stand and 'promenade' (hence the name).

One evening, as I sat high up in the gods (a more expensive ticket: my legs weren't prepared to go the whole way) and listened to the decades-old 'heave ho' ritual from the crowd as the grand piano lid was lifted for the evening's concert, a wave of tenderness washed over me. For this magnificent, odd, tough, eccentric country. England *is* great. Mighty. Open. Forgiving. I was snagged by emotion when *I Vow to Thee My Country* began and the chorus swelled and the entire audience joined in. When under attack England creaks and groans, but stands firm. Gloriously firm. It always has.

> It's their anger that has made them,
> arguably, over the long run, the most
> consistently successful of the old
> European nations, certainly the most
> inventive and adventurous and energetic.
> Controlled anger is a great impetus to
> achievement. You have to do something
> with it. Anger simply won't let you be
> comfortable in your own skin.
>
> AA Gill, on the English

No, the English aren't comfortable in their own skin. They're not by nature warm and enthusiastic and welcoming, but I've made some of the dearest friends of my life in this country. Just a handful, but a handful is a treasure trove indeed.

And there is so much beauty in the land. Sea softening into sky in Cornwall, the golden light of Gloucestershire, a mist-wrapped Edinburgh. A simple word like 'nine' that the Glaswegians can put so much colour into — I just want to drink their lilt. A house for sale in the local paper in Winchester advertising a floor made of thatchers' ladders and coffin lids. A writer's cottage in Cornwall I sometimes disappear to that's older than white settlement in Australia, which has foot-wide floorboards salvaged from shipwrecks. A rose-covered stone house we've escaped to in Hardy's West Country with a Roman villa under one of its fields. The wonder of snowfall in Wales, soaking up sound. Walking through a London fog at four am and holding out my hand, wondrous: it's like soft, still rain. Bath Abbey: a skeleton of stone and its flesh, light. Scottish mountains nudging the roof of the sky, the silence a presence in that place.

An English friend says Australia seems so messy to her: 'Because of all the overhead wires — we don't have them like you do. Your country towns seem so untidy. The barbed wire for fences, all of that.' Ah yes, indeed, compared to the beautiful stone walls that stitch the English blankets of green.

I see all that beauty, all of it, gulp it up, but it's not locked in my heart. And that's why the UK will never quite hold me. (Although it sometimes comes close. For example, when I overheard a woman asking her friend if she'd like a cup of tea from her Thermos as we all sat rugged up on a pebbly English beach, watching kelp-heavy waves heaving their load. 'Yes,' I thought, smiling, 'yes I *would* like a cup of tea. Very much.')

'Home'. Such a loaded word. Especially when the relentless gypsy within has pulled me from place to place for so long, obscuring my sense of where home actually is. Your daddy and I are teasing each other now in our conversations, with *where* we could possibly live, *if* we ever returned: both reluctant to declare Sydney or Melbourne, the cities we've each spent most of our lives in. Two places that belong to one or the other of us too much.

All I know now is that I want to be buried on Australian soil. I dread dying in the continent where the cold curls up in my bones, and being laid to rest in it. But I'm so grateful for the challenging, exhilarating, frustrating expatriate experience, for the texture it's given both our lives — a richness we wouldn't have had by floating, restlessly, in the comfort zone of 'home'.

PART SIX

67

Whenever I return to Australia I'm struck by the brutality of the land. It seems so *hostile* to non-Indigenous humans, in comparison with benign England. Imagine what those first European settlers must have felt — used to their soft rain and bucolic hills. It hits me now every time I go back to Australia: this land is not meant for us. And it will not be beaten. The foliage is spiky and hard and prickly and shardy. The sun is penetrating. The skies are dramatic. The rain pummels, and that's when it comes. When it does it can bring floods, fast. Or hailstones the size of golf balls. There are cyclones and earthquakes, avalanches of snow, droughts. And of course, fire.

It's an intrinsic part of our continent. Many native species of plants only seed and flower after fire. The Aboriginal people know that. They've used it for thousands of years; understand its regenerative qualities. They've learned to sensibly exploit it and know how to use it sparingly (I've been laughed at several times by Aboriginal people with my attempts to make a campfire — always too big and abundant, wasting too much fuel — whereas theirs are invariably small, neat, economical and intense).

This land will not be tamed. Europeans may have settled the continent but cannot, ever, completely bend it to their will. Especially when it comes to fire — demonstrated so shockingly on 7 February 2009. Black Saturday. Australia's greatest natural disaster, which left 173 people dead and 7,500 homeless in country Victoria.

As Aussie kids we're taught to be wary of fire. We're instructed about the best methods of surviving it; we all know the bushfire warning signs in country areas; all know of the volunteer fire brigades. For many young people in the bush it's a rite of passage to join up.

And we're a people spellbound by fire — who hasn't been intoxicated by the smell of it, somewhere, distant on the breeze? In 1988 a series of ceremonial bonfires was lit for the Bicentenary. The historian, Geoffrey Blainey, said the event was honouring 'the most powerful, majestic and frightening force in our history: the force of fire'. Patrick White, in his novel *Tree of Man*, wrote, 'there were very few who did not succumb to the spell of the fire. They were swayed by it, instead of it by them'.

That's the point: we are swayed by it when we should be ever vigilant, ever wary, when so many of us live in such volatile places. In houses — nay, entire country towns — surrounded by huge payloads of fuel: those glorious gum trees with their eucalyptus oil that burns like sump oil when alight. We should rightly be seduced by the beauty of this land — but not seduced so that we lose all sense.

An outsider recognised the bushfire's destructive potency: HG Wells visited Australia in the late 1930s and wrote, 'a bushfire is not an orderly invader, but a guerrilla'. Yes. We cannot always read its tactics, and we cannot always defeat it.

68

On Black Saturday the flames were goaded by one-hundred-kilometre winds and temperatures pushing 47°C. It was the perfect scenario for a disaster: a once-in-a-century heatwave and fierce winds riding the back of a protracted drought. The bush was tinder dry, and it was in difficult-to-access locations. Humans didn't stand a chance as the mighty, untameable continent roared once again. I was with my kids in our cottage at the time; we watched, speechless with horror, as the extent of the destruction dawned on the nation.

Scott Edwards of Narbethong: 'It sounded like one thousand jumbo jets taking off ... the ground started shaking and windows started rattling ... I looked up at the sky at one point and all I could see was demons.' Others describe the fire as roaring like an express train and travelling as fast.

The fires flashed through gullies of Messmate Stringybark, Grey Box, White Gum and Blue Gum. Hanging strips of Stringybark acted as ladders for the flames and the huge quantities of Blue Gum oil created billowing black smoke. It was like a 1970s disaster movie; people described it as apocalyptic, a war zone; one elderly man said it was worse than the German bombing in World War II.

Kinglake, one of the towns hardest hit, felt in hindsight like a firetrap waiting to happen. A place built in the middle of a national park. House upon house; right up in the trees. What hope did the poor buggers have?

The shocking, stilling savagery of it. Victims found huddled together, clinging; tight groups of friends and families and strangers. The area attracted tree changers — a lot were young families with young kids opting for a cheaper, greener, simpler life. Young people, old people, children, babies died in their bathrooms. Their baths. Their backyards and driveways. In makeshift cellars under their houses where they choked from lack of oxygen. Beside their motorcycles and in their exploding cars as they tried to escape.

I'm haunted by the image of the four incinerated cars that collided in smoke impossible to see through. Imagine the terror of those final minutes. Seconds. Entire families.

Triple zero operators listened to people dying over the phone. More than 4,200 emergency calls were made from people trapped. On the innocence of an Australian Saturday afternoon, a day reserved for lawnmowers and weddings.

St Andrews. Churchill. Kinglake. Marysville. Kilmore and Clonibane. The names speak of their British heritage. In Marysville, at the foothills of the mythic Snowy Mountains, at least one fifth of the population perished. All that was left of it was a wasteland of ash and crumpled tin and a few brick chimneys.

The fire came so quickly. The heat was so intense. Paint peeled off bonnets, cars melted, hub caps turned into rivers of silver lava. Door handles were too hot to grab, even with gloves. Bricks were shattered and window glass melted, as did the soles of shoes as people ran. Some made it, some didn't. Houses were literally cremated. Household fridges — which we're told withstand nuclear blasts — folded in on themselves like wet cardboard. People were burned beyond recognition; some will never be identified.

And as these fires were consuming everything in their path in the nation's south, in the north floods were ruining homes on the tropical Queensland coast.

This land. My country. Once again it had roared.

69

Firefighter John Munday had to save his crew by leaving the beleaguered town of Marysville. He spoke movingly afterwards of seeing a young father, with his two young boys, in the middle of the street, wearing light clothes and a look of bewilderment, just … standing there.

Standing there, as the fire came.

Lest we forget. All the people who have gone, but especially the children. And remember those kids who have witnessed sights no person should ever have to witness in their life. God help them.

In the thick of despair, so many stories of resilience and ingenuity and courage and hope, and once again, they're quintessentially Australian stories. 'I love you. I'm proud of you. Work hard,' said a woman over the phone to her kids with what she thought were her final words.

Black Saturday showed Australia at its worst, and best, and for all the horror I'm glad you boys were living here to experience what it is to be Australian in the shocked aftermath. Movingly, the entire nation united to support its fellow Aussies. Prime Minister Kevin Rudd announced there would be rebuilding 'brick by brick'. Because of course, that is the Australian way.

Donations of money, goods and services from across the nation were staggering. At faraway little Coal Point Public we were asked to find items like blankets and toys and toiletries, and later had a dress-up day where the kids had to donate a gold coin. Everyone rallied, everyone rose to the task.

'We are new residents in Australia and our hearts are truly humbled by what we have seen,' wrote Vicki from Forest Lake, Queensland, on the *Daily Telegraph*'s public message page. 'The love, kindness, generosity and compassion that Australians have shown during this time are second to none. We have seen such a wonderful community spirit, coupled with sheer determination to survive and so much hope that we are proud to call Australia home.'

70

Yet as with so many of Australia's natural disasters, what also follows is a spirited slanging match. Townies versus country people; the East Coast elite versus everyone else. Step forward the 'shiny bum experts' (as Steve Price so eloquently called them) at their computer screens, who professed to have all the answers. 'Use your time to make people feel better about themselves — not worse,' Mr Price admonished.

'Life or lifestyle,' warned a fire chief. Blame? The tree changers who wanted their pretty views. The Greenies who wanted endangered animals protected. The councils for not letting people clear trees from their properties. Remove the fuel, burn it off; Aboriginal people have known this for thousands of years. Isn't it common sense? Back and forth it went, as it always does.

'Stay or go?' became the question of the day. The examples of the US and Canada were looked at, where the policy is evacuation and by force if necessary. 'Fight or flee?' became a fascinating question of gender. Most commonly it was the mothers and wives — the homemakers — who chose to lose the lot rather than risk lives. More often the blokes wanted to stay and fight, sometimes with tragic consequences, not just for themselves but the people attached to them. In Australia a man's house is his castle — but at what cost?

Then after all the yakking and slanging and mudslinging there was Kevin Rudd's strong and clear and impassioned speech at the memorial service a few weeks later. It spoke of his humble origins in a Queensland dairy town. He knows this country and its people, he's from its heartland, and he knows how to speak to them.

'Simply know this: you who suffer are not alone. This great Australian family is with you … In some countries, tragedy exposes the fault lines in a nation. The strong abandoning the weak; one region indifferent to the sufferings of another, one culture uncaring as to the needs of the other. But ours is a different nation. Our nation has been as one. Australia is a nation of compassion.'

The spirit that made Australia great is personified by nine-year-old Nadeesha Pallegedera, from Denistone East Public School in Sydney. She walked into her principal's office and struggled to lift a very large tin moneybox out of her school bag. Inside were her entire life savings. 'It's money for the children of the fire,' she said. She didn't know how much was in there but she explained, 'I've been saving it all my life.'

Inside that box was $457.53 and two pennies. Principal Warren Poole said later, 'Then she zipped up her bag, smiled, and quietly left the office.' He added, 'Do they come any better?' Nadeesha was born in Australia and has Sri Lankan parents. Such a fabulously Aussie story, and such an inspiring one.

A week after the fires a breeze broke the back of the heat. Then the rains came, pummelling the earth hard, for days and days. 'It's God crying over the bush fires, Mummy,' you, Lachie, said. An Aboriginal person told me once that when a great spirit dies a big wind comes, a storm, whipping through everything and blowing it all clean. That's what it felt like. Repairing the world, regenerating, moving on. Australia's good at that.

7 1

... having served under that bright sky you
may look up
    but don't ask too much:
some cold beer, a few old friends in the
afternoon,
    a southerly buster at dusk.

John Tranter, 'Backyard'

Something else struck me about the fires; something
intrinsically Australian. The spirit of mateship. That's not
just mateship among friends, but mateship within the
wider community. You're an Aussie, so you're my mate, and
I'm going to help you out.

It's the spirit that draws me in London when I come
across an Australian nanny at my kids' nursery and
befriend her rather than her boss; when I fall into chatting
at Heathrow with some old-aged pensioners from Broken
Hill; that has me inviting around for dinner the friend of a
friend who's visiting London for the first time. It's the spirit
that has me laughing with the people around me on the

Sydney bus when they driver has a go at me for not storing my stroller properly. It's the spirit that bowls over a Polish exchange student visiting Lake Macquarie: 'Everyone says hello, even if they don't know you.' It's the spirit that puts a smile in your talk; that loosens and lightens you; that teaches you kindness and tolerance and a fair go for everyone; and I want you children to have it.

Once a week, if you've been good, you're allowed a tuck-shop order at Coal Point Public. It's a highly anticipated treat. Every Friday I find myself giving you a couple of extra dollars. 'For your mates. Buy something for them. It's the Aussie way, OK? Mates are important.' Because my brothers still have friends from their childhood whom they're fiercely loyal to, and I want you boys to have something of that too. You need to know the lovely ways of Aussie mateship, the qualities attached to it that will carry you through life: loyalty, trust, honour, integrity, compassion, warmth.

Years ago I ripped out a scrap from the *Sydney Morning Herald*'s legendary 'Column Eight'. For me, it sums up the concept of mateship:

'The spirit that made Australia great. A nine-year-old from Queanbeyan West Public School decided last week he wanted a haircut. To the dismay of the barber, he kept asking for his hair to be cut shorter and shorter, until he was almost bald. His parents decided the boy would have to live with the cut — he was not allowed to wear a hat [*those were the days*] and was told he would have to face the ridicule of his schoolmates. Face them he did — in fact, he charged them 5c each to run their hands over the bristle, made $2.65, and bought five Paddle Pops for himself and his mates.'

Translate that Queanbeyan schoolyard to an English one and to me, the story just doesn't work. Then there's this from Professor Stephen Muecke, writing in the *Australian Book Review.*

'We still don't know how much we value as Australian style might have been learned over the years from our black mates: a certain way of walking (even squatting, as the French anthropologist Marcel Mauss observed of Australians during World War I, making themselves comfortable in the trenches for hours); yarning as oral tradition and Henry Lawson's narrative style; the easy laugh; the sense of social obligation and loyalty to non-immediate family implied through the kinship system of "mates"; the rule that the only way to share is equally — in what other country does the school kid share her musk stick by breaking it and giving *her friend* the choice?'

Mateship is a code of behaviour that is caring and easy and effortless and selfless and I love Australia for it. It's why a lot of us will have overseas visitors sleeping on our couches even though the favour won't necessarily be returned, why we'll invite strangers to a party, and why the nation pulled together so superbly after Black Saturday. It's also why the ugliness of those flag-draped people on Australia Day feels so shockingly un-Australian.

Perhaps the concept of mateship developed because the working class and the underclass were such an intrinsic part of white settlement, and those people had to stick together — unite against their bosses and protect each other — and had to draw humour from their grim circumstances. Perhaps it developed because this land is so bloody tough; if we can't bond, and help each other out, and find something to laugh about while we're at it, well, we're buggered.

'Whatever sanctifies itself draws me,' Les Murray wrote in his poem 'The Hoaxist'. Mateship draws me, and all the qualities that illuminate the term: generosity and warmth, laughter and lightness, love.

The Italian designer Emilio Pucci was the first of his family to work in one thousand years — such a fabulously European story, and such a non-Australian one. I need the Aussie work ethic. I was raised among it, most of my family adheres to it, and I want to pass it on. I want you children raised with it.

Shortly after the Australia Day ructions, when the Southern Cross symbol was hijacked as an emblem of ugly, unthinking nationalism, builder Scott Cam (he had presented the TV show *Domestic Blitz* and was discovered in a pub) explained why he has the constellation tattooed on his back: 'It instils in me a sense of morality — knowing what it stands for gives you some ethics. It's that symbol of working hard, helping your mate and slogging it out without complaining.'

Pulling your weight, getting the job done, getting stuck in there, not mucking about, giving it your best shot, not giving up, going the extra mile, standing by your mates. All of that.

It's about starting bright and early — eight, or half-past, or crisply at nine — as opposed to England's leisurely ten am. Perhaps it has something to do with the southern light, the fierceness of it, waking you early; that sliver of brightness stealing through the curtains.

It's also about just having a go. You, Lachie, had your first ever school swimming carnival at Coal Point. You learn to swim in London's Kensington in a four-metre-long pool, against a wave machine. You entered yourself in the twenty-five-metre freestyle race without having a clue how long that distance was or, more importantly, if you could actually complete it. 'Just give it your best shot, that's the Aussie way,' I told you, with a hug of pride that you'd got as far as entering. The school had two teachers in their rashies standing in the middle of the pool in case anyone got into trouble.

You did give it your best shot, Lachs. You came third. And I'll never forget the smile on your face at the end of it. 'I'm an Aussie boy now, Mummy,' you said with glee. Yes, I thought, yes. We're all changing in this place.

7 3

My dad has recently been working down the pit again. Night shifts, at seventy-four. After years doing other things. He needs the money. 'They said if I could pass the medical the job's mine.' He did. 'I'll die working,' he told me years ago. He's happiest when he's working, so we leave him to it.

On days off he drives us up the Hunter Valley, past the remnants of the first pit he worked in, at Paxton, when he was sixteen. Past the first pub he drank in. Down a dirt road and past the tiny miner's cottage, in a cluster of four in the middle of the bush, that he spent most of his childhood in (at 'Stocky' — Stockrington 2 — another old mine long abandoned). Past the old house at Kearsley that his mother and father built with their bare hands in the early 1930s. They had help from my grandmother's brother, who'd arrive each day on his bicycle carrying just a hammer and a tape measure. Dad was born in the house.

One day the new owners caught us taking photos outside and invited us in. Dad told them about the cylinder detail on the top of the verandah posts: old bread tins filled with concrete. The owners were tickled pink. There were just four rooms when Dad was a kid. 'We found the old horsehair plaster,' we were told. The tiny house is now guarded by a blue cattle dog called Banjo and a red cattle dog called Ember. I loved the sheer Australianness of it all, the bush simplicity, the craft and care in its doorframes, floorboards, shelves, windows.

There's something magnificent about the Aussie spirit that refuses to be eroded by failure or hardship, that Dad 'n' Dave settler mindset. Persistence is everything, and tenacity, and ingenuity. I see it in the vigour of the old bush antiques that I often can't resist: a chest of drawers from Alice made out of kerosene tins, a Darwin bookshelf from Depression-era fruit boxes, a kitchen dresser from the Hunter Valley made of odd bits of driftwood hammered together with convict nails, with cotton reels for knobs on its drawers. I love the singular energy of all the pieces; they jump out of a room, whatever room they're in. Particularly in England, which has nothing like them. They tell stories of living hard on the land, and surviving, and there's a tough Aussie beauty in all of them.

74

Every time we head 'up the valley' with my father we swing by the cemetery at Kurri Kurri where my pop, Dad's dad, is buried. He was in coal mining for much of his life and all around us are the graves of men killed in accidents down the pit — it says so on their tombstones. Pop lived until ninety-six. His secret? A bowl of porridge every morning and 'a serene life, just let it all go love, let it go', he said toward the end.

You boys are obsessed by the grave; ask Grandfather Bob to take you again and again so you can decorate its simple plaque with pine cones and gum leaves and talk to Poppy even though you, Ollie, never met him, and you, Lachie, were a toddler when he passed away. I'm not sure why you're pulled so strongly to his resting place; perhaps it's an anchor, perhaps it gives you some kind of belonging, of continuity. And that breaks my heart. Because for your whole lives you've had your parents' uncertainty about home around you, and perhaps, finally, you've found a sense of place. And you want to nurture it, and hang on to it.

Dad tells us about his five classmates, his gang, who all left school between fourteen and sixteen to work down the pit. One was killed at forty-two in a mine accident, the others all went on to become millionaires. 'One of them, when asked by his school teacher to name two days of the week beginning with T, said Today and Tomorrow.' Dad chuckles. 'No flies on him.' The secret to their success? 'Hard work.'

'There are three types of people — those that do, those that watch those that do, and those that criticise those that do. It's best to be a do-er,' ex-Qantas chairperson, Margaret Jackson, said. I want you kids to be do-ers. To have that spirit of curiosity and quest within you; the grit to get you through life.

Freud is right. All we need is love and work, and there's such infinite pleasure in a job well done. 'When I am painting I feel happy and I let the feeling take hold of my hand,' the Aboriginal artist Fiona Omeenyo said. I feel that too, when I'm writing. It's why I have to keep working around motherhood, in whatever time I can. Because then the happiness filters through into everything else.

7 5

Now, under the gum trees, the rush to words.

Write as if you're dying, used to be my mantra to gallop me on; now, it's *write because soon you'll be back.* In Blighty, boxed back up within my proper life. And London is too noisy to write solidly in, too fractious and demanding and distracting. Here, in Lake Macquarie, I have blessed quiet.

I do a lot of driving in Australia; good, long, thinking driving; not aggressive London tooting and ducking and weaving. I have relaxed into a life of simplicity here and it feels so invigorating. This trip has saved me. The writer in me is uncurling again, after years of crammed motherhood, and it's giving me strength.

They're dangerous, these simple, temporary, golden-hued days. Because I want to stay within them. As our return date approaches a balloon of sadness is settling over me: I don't want to let go of this.

Once, it was: *write before the naysayers and the sneerers fool you into giving up.* 'Waste of time, that,' said my beloved dad when I first told him, twenty years ago, that I wanted to give novel-writing a go. Because it wasn't a proper job, because it wouldn't give me a good living, because it was 'arty' and blimey where did that come from, love? Dad was only the start. Australia doesn't treat its writers well; if I'd wanted affirmation I should have lived in France.

'To be nobody but yourself in a world which is doing its best, night and day, to make you like everybody else — means to fight the hardest battle which any human can fight, and never stop fighting,' said E E Cummings.

I lost the urge in the thick of early marriage, those heady days of delight and then the intense years of tiny babies, milky and mewly with want. 'I forgot all my wild, unattainable ambitions in the little pleasures of everyday life. Such a thing as writing never entered my head,' Miles Franklin wrote in *My Brilliant Career*. Oh yes.

In London I work now in stolen moments while you children are asleep or at school or with babysitters. I've annexed a new writing life of short chapters and snatched thoughts, of three-line paragraphs and fragments on shopping dockets and bills, for I never get a long stretch of time to myself. Gone are the fourteen-hour writing sessions fuelled by champagne and chocolate; the luxury of sixty drafts; the week-long sojourns in distant cottages with Andy protesting, 'You're leaving me for a book.'

I've been distracted, euphorically, over the past eight years by a cherished man and you kids and I haven't seen things as sharply or as clearly; I'll take up the pen and write in bursts then put it down again when another deliciousness, another baby comes along. It's now a fumbling, halting kind of working life; deadlines have slipped away, sometimes whole books. Once it would take six months to fill a journal with observations and story ideas and thoughts, now it takes four years.

But then the will comes back. And here I am now, in our little fibro shack with you kids bouncing around me. Here I am gleaning time to work, stealing it, from all of you. Snatching a precious few hours here and there and just gunning it. Gunning it. Ha, haven't said that in all my London years and now it's slipped back into my vocabulary like a fly at a barbie.

Here I am with no distractions like school runs and Starbucks and bills to pay and being a wife, a good wife; and not being able to say no, to so many requests, from so many people, such a lot of the time. 'I feel a real horror of people closing over me,' Katherine Mansfield wrote in her journal in 1914, and I feel that too.

I want to be a woman who radiates serenity, that is my ambition now. Because from serenity flows so much: happiness, compassion, patience, trust, grace. When I'm writing — when I'm doing what I really want to do in life — I have a quietness of the soul. It shelters me, and Andy knows it. He has given me this freedom for three months and I am so grateful for it. For him.

As I get older I'm becoming more chuckly, looser, lighter. Dwelling within the vast delight of family; simplifying; paring back; not needing so much clutter around me. Noise or people or meetings or things, mainly things. All that *stuff.* I want to be good at being alive. I need to improve. The journey never stops.

Another woman is starting. I've found a new one, and I want to take her back to London with me. If I can.

PART SEVEN

The days are galloping now; the cold is tingeing our April mornings. Soon we must leave. I will return to London scrubbed of restlessness, sated; but I'm not sure how long the stillness will last.

Pablo Neruda said the frontier elected him, and I feel like that too; and there's an eternal yearning and despair because of it: it's such a selfish, incorrigible want. I'd love to stay here in this simple life, head further bush, pare my world back even more to just dust and road and sky and light. There's a desert chick inside me who refuses to let go.

But I'm a mother now, and a wife. London calls. The crammed, built-up world we've created for ourselves.

Several years ago I was in Lorne, on the Victorian coast, for an extremely rare writing sojourn; Andy and you boys were with his parents. It was raining and the bush reached down to the sea and in the air the smell of eucalyptus and wet was mixing with the tang of salt and somewhere the remnants of a bushfire and I breathed it in deep, intoxicated, and unfurled my true self. It was as if I could feel again, being there, alone, in that beautiful place. I was writing again, too; doing, creating. I needed it strongly at that time in my life. 'What is marriage doing to me?' I wrote in my journal back then. 'Losing me? And here I am with that dangerous feeling that I have to crash catastrophe into my life.'

With *this* trip, in a small way, I did. Now I'm on the cusp of reuniting with my husband after three months' time out. I am absolutely ready: cleaned, stilled, refreshed. It also feels like we can renegotiate the terms of the relationship; be clearer and firmer with each other, more open; say what isn't working and what we're sick of. This trip has been about regaining a measure of control in some way.

It's taken this break to realise the extent of my love for Andy. I'm as excited as a child for his return to us, can't wait for him to see the kids; changed, brightened under this Aussie sunshine. To see *him*. Rested. (Can't wait to throw you kids at him and sleep!)

The thought of him fills me up. But so does Australia. This book feels like not only a love letter to my country, but to my husband.

It's why, after all, I'm heading back.

7 7

This trip has decided me: I want to move back to the light. A Judith Wright snippet of poetry has haunted me all through my years of exile: 'My days burn with the sun.' All three of you children have grown to love this outdoor life, living under the thumb of its weather. 'Thea will be an outside girl when she grows up,' you, Lachie, said recently. Yes. Because even as a toddler she craves it; cries and wriggles in protest when I pluck her from the fresh air and bring her back into the house. Just like her mum.

And you boys have revelled in the great outdoors. You're so proud of the tiny freckles that have appeared on your noses despite all my best efforts. To me, you kids are lively here as in full of life, and it makes my heart sing. You can run; you have space; you've instinctively seized the possibility within it and Australia has welcomed it. You've become bigger in your time here, sparkier, tougher, more resilient.

You certainly know what a mozzie looks like now and are worryingly eager to track down a funnel-web. 'Is that one, Mummy? Is that one?' When you first came to Lake Macquarie you both shied away in horror at an old cicada shell; now, you're collecting crabs from the lake with your bare hands. You're learning Aussie self-sufficiency, nous, practicality, and your soft little London feet are toughening up.

I want you boys to grow up with the sweetness that I love in the Australian male, and the humour, and the generosity of spirit; and I want you, Thea, to grow up among those glorious Aussie chicks who are sparky and strong and self-sufficient — all without losing their femininity.

But is it better here? Would an English person feel as I do or am I just hopelessly biased? The rent-a-car manager I've been hiring a vehicle from in Newcastle has a firm opinion. He's from England's north, and he's had a son in Australia, now six. I tell him he should be doing what I'm doing in reverse: taking his boy across to England, back to his own family, and putting him into a local school for a term.

'But by coming here you've taken your kids to the better place,' he says simply. 'It doesn't work as well for me, doing it the other way around. It's not as good.'

Andy arrives. We are all ready for it. Brimming with excitement to see him, barely able to sleep the night before he flies in, zooming with happiness.

For the next three weeks he lives the Aussie life. Drinks his beer on verandahs at dusk, reads his papers by pools, settles in to the computerised luxury of our brand new, hired Commodore. ('Isn't this fabulous? It's like driving from your loungeroom.' To me, after our compact European car, it's so big it's like driving a tank.) He drops the boys off to Coal Point Public in the morning, chuckling at the familiarity of it all: he, once, attended a school just like this. He attends parent–teacher meetings and is as impressed as I am with the teachers; yarns with Ms Cressy; makes it to the Easter Bonnet Parade and family picnic, wolfing down the sausage sangers and yakking with the other dads; he giggles with glee at the sight of his Notting Hill wife behind the tuck-shop counter (those Aussie mums have the measure of me as soon as I walk into the kitchen. While the other two helpers set themselves the task of zealously cooking the Anzac biscuits and pikelets and chicken for the burgers, I'm assigned to … sandwiches. Yep. One look at me is all it takes.)

There's so much laughter in our time here. I love seeing the easy, respectful way Andy takes my grandmother, Win, by the elbow, love seeing him commune with elderly people (they're never in our London world). 'I need one of these!' he exclaims as he brings her her walking frame. Love the way he joshes with my dad when he's asked if he's 'thrown me into the Thames yet'. Chuckle as he wanders the supermarket aisles, exclaiming over all the delights from his youth: Milo, fresh flavoured milk, Mint Slices, Drive washing powder. Applaud as the man with the beautifully cut London suits buys a pair of King Gee shorts 'because they're comfortable, OK?'; and can't resist some Baby Blunnies for his beloved girl. He's constantly asked to cook the barbie, it becomes a running joke, as if all around him people are attempting to fold him back into Aussie life (and he acquits himself damn well). So much warmth, so much affectionate delight in him being back.

We fly up to Cairns for a week to stay with his parents and I watch him — like myself previously on this trip — uncurling. Chuckling, lightening. Among family and fresh air, under a tall sun and blue sky and surrounded by all the familiarities of childhood. The old biscuit tin, corned beef, Passiona, the table that's been with his parents his entire life, the forty-year-old casserole dish, faded photos, board games he played himself as a child.

We talk of sending you boys on a plane by yourselves when you're older — if we lived in Australia — to stay with Granny and Grandpa. You've done it already with my father on this trip, as has Thea, and it worked splendidly; it was a struggle wresting you all back. I look at you now, Ollie, playing Battleship with your grandpa as I write these final chapters on the wide Queensland verandah; I look at Thea with a dustpan having a ball with Granny as she cleans up, and the gladness fills my heart. Tonight you boys are going on a sleepover on Grandpa's boat, just the four men of the family, and you've already gone with Daddy to buy your midnight feast. Who was the most excited? Daddy, of course. Because he was let loose among all the sweets of his youth, and he wanted you boys to love them too. Grandpa is thrilled, too; to have all his boys in his life, and it's such a rare occurrence; every couple of years at the most. And that, now, is breaking my heart.

I'm so close to my grandmothers because my own childhood memories are gilded by stays with them, by myself, often: those grown-ups who loved me but didn't hassle me, who talked to me in a different way from my parents, who spoilt me — fed me Vegemite and melted butter on white bread toast and gave me Coca-Cola as a treat and tucked me into flannelette sheets with the electric blanket on — who *understood*. It was like a secret world

233

between us, one which parents weren't allowed into, and you three children are experiencing something similar to it now on this trip. I want that to be nurtured.

Andy too. And as I write this my heart's beating fast; my eyes are prickling up.

Because he has changed. There's been a seismic shift. On this trip. In these short weeks he's said yes, let's get them home. At McDonald's, of all places. Which we go to more than once while we're here, because we trust the Aussie beef — something we've never quite done in post-mad-cow England. You boys are running barefoot around the play area with your Happy Meal toys; you, Thea, have got more of your milkshake on the floor than in your cup; and in the midst of it Andy points to the packaging: 'I'm Lovin' It.'

Eh?

'Let's go back. For their schooling,' he says. 'We've always known we'll go home; we want the boys to be Aussie men. It's time.' He laughs. 'I'm loving it.'

It's so many things, I guess: seeing the ease of the way you children have slotted into your Aussie lives; the fabulous sense of space and width you're all plunging into; the zippy little swimmers suddenly around him, the confident way you boys dive and duck and weave underwater like dolphins now; your new, taut little bodies that look like they've been basted in honey; the fabulous, free school (we know we've been lucky there); the fresh air, the optimism, the blue skies; the familiarity of so much of it; the sheer weight of all your happiness here, the great swell of it; and seeing a new wife in this place.

We've never lived in Australia as husband and wife and Andy's discovered a different woman on this trip — the woman he fell in love with, years ago, the one who in a way has been lost. Over the years, with the grind of daily life, rubbed out.

79

When Andy declares his willingness to come back, well, in an instant I feel the chains — the ones that have been riveted about my chest for so long, so many weighted years — snap. I can breathe again, feel freed. The prospect of Australia again, for all of us! The prospect of flinging sun into our lungs. A bloom of strength to our walking. Feeling tall again, straightened by the light.

My beloved Anglophile recognises it's time. He's a dad now. His parents can no longer fly to see us; his father is too elderly. And there's been so much love thrown at his children in Australia, which has been so moving to witness. You've experienced a great swamping of love from grandparents, cousins, uncles, aunts, great-grandparents. After so many years, whole lifetimes, of not knowing the joy of so much love on tap.

We think it would be good to get you kids back to Australia before you, Lachie, have to start high school in England. If you did, it would then be too hard to extricate you — you'd be on the path to being British. We would spend the next twenty-odd years in England and most likely retire there and die there, because all our children would have lost their connections to Australia. So it's decided: we pull out in the next couple of years or not at all. We haven't worked out exactly when — maybe eighteen months, maybe sooner — but the important thing is that the decision is made.

As soon as it has, London — the idea of it — ceases to be a prison and becomes a playground. I'm happy to return now to Notting Hill and revel in all the lovelinesses of that life. Because I know, finally, I will not be living forever in the place I'm not meant to be living in, and I am at peace. Everything relaxes and lightens. I think the euphoria has something to do with finally, finally, being in control. After twelve years of uncertainty there is this certainty: an end date. It's all it took.

Tagore wrote, 'at once I came into a world wherein I recovered my full being'. That's how I feel. The circle is completed. The tension of exile, the great unanswered question of return, is finally answered.

But of course there will be new weights to face: family responsibilities most of all. For years I've avoided them, breezing in for a brief cup of tea every couple of years then dashing away, not really up to speed with all the day-to-day machinations of familial life. I've crammed my days with so much else; now, it will all have to be faced. I have to grow

237

up. 'Exile is in the end an act of self-concealment,' Mary Gordon wrote. Facing home again, I have to confront what I've been running from for so long: myself.

But I know now that going home is about a deepening, on so many levels; a connection with the tendrils of all the living that has informed me, stretching back to early childhood. It's about a deepening of responsibility, of morality, of aging, a 'giving back'. It's time, as simple as that, and I must act upon it.

8 0

We fly back to Newcastle briefly before we leave for England and I gulp the vividness of our final few days in Australia. The thick smell of eucalyptus and the light at six-thirty in the morning weaving its magic. The birds waking us, so many, the great raucous song of them. The hurting light of midday. The smell of a freshly mown lawn under a sharp blue sky. The exquisite relief of a cool breeze through the gums, breaking the back of the heat. The land softening as night comes stealing in. Those long lean shadows you never get in England. Dusk encroaching on the world like a thin film of milk. Leaning my head out the car window like a dog and breathing in deep the thick briny sea air. Marvelling at the vaulting sky above us, the clouds running away, the moon racing. The searing tug of the Southern Cross.

I am hostage to all of it, all.

It is time to stop the running, to chisel out the restlessness. Now, ahead, is the familiar, the known, and for the first time in my adult life I'm ready for it. My new landscape will be the children's skin, and that is how it will be for some time and I am happy, so happy, with that.

So to the beautiful lightness of aging. As you learn to let go; to accept what you cannot change and be grateful for what you can; as you revel in chuff. You children have done it to me. For with kids, your heart is flung open.

And here, on this final, free day in our little Lake Macquarie cottage (thanks to the boundless grace of Greg and Ilse), there is the smell of late gardenias wafting in on the beautiful breeze and I fling wide the windows and let in the sky and think of the grace of this settling.

I feel strong, righted. Blazing life. 'You are in heaven, aren't you?' enquires a girlfriend in Switzerland in response to a euphoric e-mail. Yes.

Rain is coming now. Tapping and then drumming on the tin roof and I wait for the earth to open up to breathe it in deep. Over all my days here is a great giggly smile.

A great giggly smile.

ACKNOWLEDGMENTS

Many people have helped me with the writing of this book; to them, I am indebted. Thank you to all my glorious friends who sent me their thoughts on Aussie childhoods, past and present (I'm still giggling over some of them). Thank you to all the gorgeous girls at Harper Collins: I tip my hat to their professionalism, energy, enthusiasm and grace. Thank you to Greg and Ilse for their boundless generosity — and the ants! And thank you to my beautiful, mad, fabulous family for being there, always, through the good times and the bad — and for luring me home. (Special thanks to Trish for setting me on the right path, again and again, and for much better cooking than I could ever manage.)

Thank you to Les Murray, Gerald Stern, Ali Clunies Ross, Mary and Louis Regan, Kim Creswell, Caroline Douglas-Pennant, the office of the Prime Minister, Warren Poole and the family of Nadeesha Pallegedera, Stephen Muecke and Christopher Phipps for allowing me to reproduce excerpts from their work.

Thank you to Faber and Faber for permission to reproduce the words of TS Eliot.

Thank you to the *Daily Telegraph* for permission to reproduce various extracts.

SOURCES

Bataille, Georges, *Guilty*, Lapis Press, Los Angeles, 1988
Blainey, Geoffrey, quoted in 'Living with the embers' by
    Simon Caterson, *The Australian*, 14 February 2009
Blake, William, 'The voice of the Devil', *The Marriage of
    Heaven and Hell*, Oxford Paperbacks, London, 1975
Brontë, Charlotte, from a poem written in 1835

Cam, Scott, quoted in 'Scott Cam blitzes neo-Nazi thugs' by Nick Leys, *Sunday Telegraph*, 1 February 2009

Chekhov, Anton, 'An Anonymous Story', *Ward Number Six and Other Stories*, Oxford University Press, USA, 2008

Coward, Nöel, *Brief Encounter*, directed by David Lean, 1945

Cummings, EE, 'A Poet's Advice to Students', *A Miscellany*, Argophile Press, NY, 1958. Reproduced with permission.

Donovan, Patrick, 'Cave yearns for home', *The Age*, 20 September 2004

Engels, Friedrich, *The Condition of the Working-Class in England in 1844*, Oxford University Press, USA, 2009

Gellhorn, Martha, quoted in *Spymistress* by William Stevenson, Arcade Publishing, New York, 2006

Gill, AA, 'I hate England', *The Times*, 30 October 2005

Gopnik, Adam, 'Rewriting Nature', *The New Yorker*, 23 October 2006

Hoggart, Simon, quoted in *Australia: Biography of a nation* by Phillip Knightley, Jonathan Cape, London, 2000

James, Henry, *The Great Good Place*, Kessinger Publishing, USA, 2004

Karnikowska, Nina and Carroll, Nick, 'The Two of Us' column, *Good Weekend*, 21 March 2009. Reproduced with permission.

Mackellar, Dorothea, 'My Country', HarperCollins*Publishers*, Sydney, 1990. Reproduced by arrangement with the Licensor, the Estate of Dorothea Mackellar, c/- Curtis Brown (Aust) Pty Ltd.

Marquez, Gabriel Garcia, *Love in the Time of Cholera*, Penguin Books, London, 1989

Matthiessen, Peter, *The Snow Leopard*, Penguin Books, London, 1987

McComb, David, *Wide Open Road*, Mushroom Music Publishing. Reproduced with permission.

McKinney, Meredith and Wright, Judith, *With Love and Fury: Selected letters of Judith Wright*, National Library of Australia, 2006. Reproduced with permission.

Murray, Les, 'The Hoaxist', *The Biplane Houses*, Black Inc, Melbourne, 2006. Reproduced with permission.

Murry, John Middleton (ed), *Journal of Katherine Mansfield*, Persephone Books, London, 2006

Omeenyo, Fiona, quoted in 'The old people today are not sure about this abstraction thing' by Angela Bennie, *Sydney Morning Herald*, 18–19 August 2007

Rushdie, Salman, 'A Dream of Glorious Return', *The New Yorker*, 2000

Stern, Gerald, 'Today a Leaf', 2005. Reproduced with permission.

Tranter, John, 'Backyard', *Urban Myths: 210 Poems: New and Selected*, University of Queensland Press, St Lucia, 2006. Reproduced with permission.

Wells, John, *Rude Words: A history of the London Library*,
Macmillan, London, 1991. Reproduced with
permission.
White, Patrick, *Tree of Man*, Random House Publishers,
Sydney, 1994

Every effort has been made to contact copyright holders. If
there are any ommissions we apologise to those concerned,
and ask that they contact HarperCollins*Publishers* Australia
so that we can correct any oversight as soon as possible.